BOOKS BY

J. GREGORY CONWAY

CONWAY'S ENCYCLOPEDIA OF FLOWER ARRANGEMENT
(1957)

CONWAY'S TREASURY OF FLOWER ARRANGEMENTS
(1953)

FLOWERS: THEIR ARRANGEMENT
(1940)

FLOWERS: EAST-WEST
(1938)

These are BORZOI BOOKS
published in New York by ALFRED A KNOPF

This gorgeous design is rich with the glow of bountiful harvests. The bright yellow chrysanthemums have central petals with the tone of the red chrysanthemums; and the red flowers, in their turn, are centered with yellow. Sprays of pyracantha berries are threaded among the blossoms, complemented by a branch that arches to the table. This latter branch ties the arrangement to the table, and points the way to the one persimmon that rests against the container. Other persimmons form the central placement to unify the chrysanthemums, the berries, and the vase.

CONWAY'S
ENCYCLOPEDIA
OF
FLOWER
ARRANGEMENT

BY

J. GREGORY CONWAY

Photography by Julian Hiatt

ALFRED A KNOPF   NEW YORK

L.C. catalog card number: 57–10340

© J. Gregory Conway, 1957

THIS IS A BORZOI BOOK,
PUBLISHED BY ALFRED A. KNOPF, INC.

FOREWORD

Many books have been written on flower arrangement. What, then, can be the justification for another? The reason for issuing this one is simple: it is intended to clarify the confusing ideas that have been circulated by some of those already published.

I have reviewed the entire body of literature in the field, including my own earlier books on the subject, to ascertain the basic facts that must be known by one who wishes to work in floral art.

I have discovered that the early books were general and that most of them treated flower arrangement as a branch of art. They gave an analysis of art principles illustrated by attractive compositions of floral design. Their chief function, then, was to explain the basic patterns of arrangements for home display or any social function.

This approach was satisfactory for the readers of twenty years ago. It gave them the kind of help they needed. But the present trend is very different. We have today a far more enlightened public than the arrangers of a quarter-century ago. Activities of garden clubs, publication of small magazines, lectures and classes devoted to floral art have given the arranger a background of factual information about the plants themselves. As a result, most of the new books are highly specialized. Current publications, for the most part, are very attractive, slim volumes that discuss only one topic out of the wide range that is necessary to an understanding of floral art as it is practiced today. The beginning arranger needs all this information, but to obtain it she must purchase many books. For most people the price is prohibitive.

I have endeavored in this one volume to supply the arranger's need. I have covered the entire field of floral art, giving in brief form the theory and practical suggestions for developing basic skills. The chapters devoted to color and design supply a background of artistic principles. The discussions of foliage, fruit and vegetables, plants of distinction, and dried materials give not only a thorough presentation of their possibilities for floral design, but also a fund of information for their care, handling, and treatment. The sections covering period arrangements, holiday and fete day designs, centerpieces, containers, and accent objects discuss the background of floral design—with a wealth *of supplementary suggestions. The chapters on miniature Japanese floral art and foreseeable trends in flower arranging add completeness to the wide range of topics.*

The book, therefore, is truly an encyclopedia and is intended for two types of readers: the average person who wishes to make tasteful arrangements for the home, and the serious student of floral art who works in accordance with established principles.

I have chosen to stress in this new book the direct relationship of horticulture to flower arrangement. For that reason the opening chapter is devoted entirely to garden growth. I hope that the emphasis placed on the growing of the materials that one arranges will be of real value to the beginner; for I believe that the handling and the labor incident to the production of flowers and foliage will reveal those qualities of beauty in form, color, and texture which are needed for plant patterns.

Some of the material in this book is very similar to portions of my previous books. Repetition is inevitable, for I wish this book to be entirely comprehensive in its coverage.

I am indebted to Elinor Wallace Hiatt for her many hours of research and her invaluable creative contribution in the preparation of this book.

To Ruth Browning Zant, I extend my gratitude for outlining the chapter headings. My sister Claire and Melvin Bussey assisted me. I am very grateful to both of them.

The beautiful Empire urns used in Plate 60 were a gift from Marion and Mai Gage; and the unusual form seen in Plate 165 was discovered by Tura McWilliams in New Mexico.

J Gregary Conway

CONTENTS

viii   *Contents*

LIST OF PLATES

COLOR PLATES

CONWAY'S
ENCYCLOPEDIA
OF
FLOWER
ARRANGEMENT

CHAPTER I

A Garden Border for the Arranger

EVERY PERSON who beautifies his home with floral arrangements realizes the need for a liberal and steady source of plant material. If he must depend entirely upon purchased flowers, he learns at the outset that beauty does not come easily—it has its price. The person whose house is set within a well-kept garden, who has only to choose among the ready items and select those cuttings with which he can create a carefully wrought design, also pays. He buys his flowers with time, with energy, with the spending of strength—hours consumed in planning, in planting, in care and maintenance. He, too, knows that beauty is dearly bought.

The average homeowner today lives on a small town lot. In planting the free areas around the house, he has two purposes in mind: to beautify his surroundings and to provide flowers for the house. Very seldom does he have space for a cutting garden. Instead, he depends upon his borders for his cutting. He realizes, then, the need for careful planting.

The borders are usually edging strips. Always the four sides of the house must be considered; always the sides and the back of the lot must be planted, and sometimes the front; frequently there are paths to be rimmed. Occasionally the small lot provides space for flower beds, but the chief feature is the border.

The homeowner in his role of gardener will design his borders with the same care and thought that he gives to his arrangements. He will choose plants that are suitable for his location, that will succeed under the local conditions of the area in which they are to live, and that please his personal taste. The third of these factors, his preference, is the most important. Modern science knows how to supplement deficiencies of soil; care and hard work can overcome many difficulties of environment; but nothing can take the place of personal liking, no matter how unreasoning or unreasonable it may be.

The wise gardener will familiarize himself with the plant requirements of his location. The books on horticulture divide the country into separate sections with boundaries that have been determined by latitude and by nearness to high mountains or oceans or deserts. The gardener will learn presently that even short distances of one or two hundred miles north and south make a difference in plant development. Perhaps the most desirable time of planting will vary a week or so, or the period required for full maturity and consequent time of bloom. The temperature of the location is another circumstance to be considered. In those zones where the summers are lengthy, where there are many long days of sunshine week after week, plant reaction to prolonged warmth is as important, and may be as noticeable, as the dormancy of plants in northern latitudes. If, then, the gardener's taste demands plants that will not grow easily in his zone, he must introduce into his environment whatever compensating factors of shade or of heat may be needed to offset, in part, the difficulties that confront his vegetation.

The gardener must study the local conditions of his town lot. Each planting area will present, at least in part, a different set of problems. The nature of the soil is easily the most important factor governing plant growth. While most plants require a neutral-to-acid soil, others demand a definite alkalinity. Fortunately horticultural chemistry has found the answers to so many soil problems that the average homeowner can usually supplement any lack, and planting can proceed as desired. Next, the exposure of each border is a governing circumstance. The prevailing weather can destroy one kind of planting as surely and as quickly as it can guarantee the success of another. The range of temperature on the south side of a house will differ many degrees from that on the north side. Closely related to extremes of temperature is the amount of moisture the planting will require, and its regularity. Not quite so easy to correct as lack of moisture is the problem presented in some locations by the winds. In an area subject to strong or sudden winds, it is completely futile to plant tall, leggy, brittle plants unless careful windbreaks have been provided.

Once the gardener has investigated the local conditions and has decided to conform to them or to change them, he proceeds to the choice of materials. He plans the border in much the same manner as he plans his arrangements. He is building a design with plant material; he is manipulating color and texture; he has an eye for masses and voids in his pattern; and he considers the background against which this design will stand and the point from which it will be viewed.

The border planting is intended to improve the appearance of the house, to direct attention to important architectural features, and to hide or subdue unpleasant details of structure. Not too long ago if the plantings looked well when viewed from the front, the gardener had succeeded in his design; but the contemporary home with its great windows and walls of glass has introduced a new problem in border design. The house and its adjacent garden are now one unit; consequently the pattern must be as beautiful when viewed from within the house as it is from the more conventional point of view.

The background of the border is maintained usually with a few well-chosen shrubs. In selecting these, the gardener tries to maintain a harmony between the plant material and the house. If the building is large and the grounds spacious, then the shrubs can be strong and bold; but if the house is small, huge leaf forms seem coarse. Shrubs with smaller leaves and flowers will be more attractive. These smaller shrubs will, in addition, permit better border design—for, whenever it can be used, a small group of shrubs will be more effective than a single plant. If shrubs are to serve as background, it will take several to produce the proper strength. Three closely set, or five if they are very small, will make a noticeable group.

After the background has been decided, the gardener must make a list of the plants—and their colors—that he wants and the time when he wants them to bloom. He will remember that no plant variety in a border is isolated. Behind it, beside it, in front of it, are other plants almost always different in color and in kind. He will, then, have in mind their form and their texture as well as their color. He will choose some flowers with spike or raceme forms, for he will need them later to establish the patterns or the lines of his arrangements. In the same way they will form strong lines of color in the border. The choice is wide:

ACANTHUS	PENTSTEMON
CANNA	PHYSOSTEGIA
CELOSIA (PLUME)	REHMANNIA
CLARKIA	SALVIA
DELPHINIUM	SNAPDRAGON
DIGITALIS	STOCK
FRANCOA	TUBEROSE
GLADIOLUS	VERONICA
KNIPHOFIA	WATSONIA
LARKSPUR	

Just as an arrangement needs a certain amount of contrast, so the border will profit by the introduction of disk or circular forms:

ANEMONE	HEMEROCALLIS
CAMELLIA	MARIGOLD
CARNATION	PEONY
CENTAUREA	PHLOX
CHRYSANTHEMUM	POPPY
COREOPSIS	RANUNCULUS
COSMOS	ROSE
DAFFODIL	SALPIGLOSSIS
DAHLIA	SCABIOSA
DAISY	STOKESIA
FELICIA	SUNFLOWER
GAILLARDIA	TULIP
GERANIUM	VINCA
GERBERA	ZINNIA
GEUM	

These two large classifications, the spike and the disk, are the only flower forms needed by the beginning arranger. Many small gardens contain little or nothing else. But extended experience brings an awareness of variations within these forms.

Circular flowers can be flat like the cosmos, the daisy, the gaillardia, and the pansy; or they can be mounded like the marigold, the fluffy aster, and the ball chysanthemum. Some circular forms grow in heads: the candytuft, the geranium, and the hydrangea. Many of them are not single blossoms. The *Compositae* have a group corolla made up of many flowers, very tiny, crowded closely together, and surrounded by a circle of rays. The popular gerbera is a good illustration of this kind of circular flower. Frequently the circle of the corolla and the calyx is bent into a cup or bell. The California poppy, the nasturtium, the single petunia, the salpiglossis, are deepened in this way. Or a part of the blossom is narrowed to form a tube or funnel. The fuchsia and the columbine are found in many gardens devoted to old-fashioned flowers. The showy iochroma and the jacobinia have brilliant tubular or trumpet-shaped blossoms. Many funnels droop upon their slender stems, and their true form is apparent only after the blossom has been lifted. The billbergia, the kniphofia, and the angel's-trumpet all nod. Flower arrangers who need a flower of particular size or shape— wide and flat, or narrow and tubular—can manipulate some blossoms to secure the desired effect. The natural form of the tulip is a partly closed bell, but a gentle pressure of the fingers opens the petals and bends them into a flat saucer.

Spike flowers also exhibit some variation in their form. The lilac grows its flowers in compact clusters at the end of a stalk. Stock, delphinium, and snapdragons crowd their flowers very closely, and the blossoms are nearly stalkless. As a result, the individual flowers are not clearly perceived unless the plant is examined, but the heavy massing produces a strong show of color. A few plants, like the hollyhock, display each blossom distinct upon the stem. The raceme of the lily of the valley is as dainty as the tiny flowers of which it is composed, because the blossoms are spaced upon the stem.

The gardener who wants novelty in flower form can secure it with the bird of paradise, the shrimp plant, some kinds of celosia, the calceolaria, and other unusual blossoms.

Whatever choice the gardener makes, the principles of planting are the same. Choose a list of important flowers that will provide a sequence of bloom. These should be set in places in the border where they will be very noticeable, a sufficient number of each to make masses that are distinctive for their color and texture. These masses are more attractive if they are oval in shape rather than square or rectangular, and if they are made up of five or more plants. The masses should be scattered at intervals the length of the border, so placed that their recurrence makes an undulating line and thus provides the rhythm of the border. The spaces between these prominent flowers may be filled with flowers of complementary colors and forms, or with flowers of the same color that differ in tone or value and thus provide variety. The purpose of the planting is to emphasize certain striking features and yet to conduct the eye from point to point the entire length of the border.

It is comparatively easy to design a border that will be effective for the short period of one season; it is quite another matter to insure a sequence of beauty throughout the year. One device for securing a continuity of bloom is to place spring flowers in the middle of the border and later blooming flowers that will make a green foreground for the middle color in the front. Then when the spring flowers are gone, those in front will have developed sufficiently not only to replace the color of the earlier blossoms but also to conceal the area where their onetime early beauty is now faded and gone.

The edging of the border is important because it is always visible. The choice of edgings is almost unlimited, from tiny, formal evergreens to loose, colorful spreading flowers. Here the gardener can set out the plants whose small blossoms are often used as fillers in arrangements and can be substituted for ferns or foliage:

AGERATUM	LOBELIA
ALYSSUM	PANSY
CANDYTUFT	PETUNIA
CINERARIA	PHLOX
CYNOGLOSSUM	TORENIA
DIANTHUS	VERBENA
LINARIA	VIOLA

Flowering shrubs not only add beauty to a permanent planting but also can afford useful material for the arrangement. Careful selection can provide an almost continuous sequence of color with tones suited to any color scheme. The evergreen shrubs do double duty by providing the permanent areas of green that form the background of the border and by the seasonal beauty of their blossoms. The bare branches of the deciduous shrubs furnish light in the dark days of winter; at the same time their slender branches trace interesting and airy patterns among their heavier companions in the border.

Evergreen

ABELIA	ERANTHEMUM
ABUTILON	ESCALLONIA
ARBUTUS	GERALDTON WAXFLOWER
AZALEA	HIBISCUS
BARBERRY	OLEANDER
BRUNFELSIA	POINSETTIA
CLERODENDRON	RHODODENDRON
CROTOLARIA	TIBOUCHINA
CYTISUS	

Deciduous or Semi-Deciduous

ABELIA	KOLKWITZIA
AZALEA	LILAC
BARBERRY	POINSETTIA
CLERODENDRON	SYRINGA
CYTISUS	TREE PEONY
FORSYTHIA	WEIGELA
HYDRANGEA	

A brief search among the varieties of a species will determine which are the evergreen and which the deciduous types.

Borders of a sort can be planted hastily. They will not be too satisfactory. They can, of course, be improved with time. The removal of plants here and there, the replanting with flowers more to one's liking, will help. But the really successful border, the garden spot that will satisfy over the months and the years, can be built only after careful study and much planning.

PLATE 1

Vegetable and fruit forms have a remarkable sculptured quality. Three sweet potatoes grouped to form a crescent are held secure on a pin-type holder. Two turnips shorn of their leafy tops complete the arrangement. The carved wooden rooster is an interesting study in line and color since his body repeats the earth tones of the vegetables and the curve of the sweet potatoes, while his plumed tail repeats the top of the lower turnip.

CHAPTER II

Design

WHENEVER YOU set plant material within a container according to a plan or pattern, you are building a floral design. You may make a faithful copy of a pictured arrangement, or use the picture as a suggestion to be modified by your own taste, or you may show your own unaided ideas. Before you attempt original creations, you should study in detail the beautiful compositions of experienced designers.

First of all you will notice line. Line is the directional path that each object of a composition traces through space. It can be the actual length from top to bottom of a stalk of plant material. Or it can be a visual path that the observer feels within the arrangement even though it may not be precisely marked out by anything tangible. In Plate 1, for example, there is no actual line from the top of the cock's head to the foretoe; yet you are as aware of the vertical as if you had laid your pencil from point to point. This imaginary line is as important to the composition as the real lines established by the floral placements. It is the instrument of rhythmic movement through the pattern, the machinery that assures a smooth and steady advance rather than a series of pulsating leaps from point to point.

Probably you will think first of vertical line, perhaps because your primary placement is usually a vertical. It is the designer's strongest line. Vigorous and virile, it reaches upward and suggests a height above toward which it aspires. Plate 2 is an excellent example of aspiration, for each pointed tip of flax carries the implication of one just beyond. Vertical line can be used to suggest force, or it can imply a deep spiritual significance. Tall,

PLATE 2

The severe dignity of this arrangement makes it suitable for placement in the modern home where the simple vertical design will harmonize with plain, flat walls and columns. The material is New Zealand flax with variegated blades, whose edges are finely striped with ivory. Though the vertical is built by repeated repetition, the complex placement is not monotonous because of its carefully patterned construction. The alternate lifting of the pointed tips, from left to right, ensures a rhythmic movement to the centered tip. Three blades, bent in loop fashion, strengthen the base; and another leaf furled around the pin-type holder completes and stabilizes the footing.

slender arrangements find many uses in the modern home. A paneled wall is a suitable background. As a partitioning device such a design suggests a narrow dividing-column. There are many ways of strengthening a vertical line. In Plate 3, which is not a vertical composition, the floral material is arranged loosely, but the spread of the branches gives an apparent weight not justified by the airiness of the design. The vertical line of the tall, slim container has been reinforced by the vertical figure set close beside it. The complex vertical—the container aided by the figure of the saint—is now of sufficient strength to support the plant material. In Plate 4 the delicacy of the vertical placement of genista is emphasized by the contrast of the strong accessories at the base. The driftwood behind the heads of yarrow, together with the two supporting figurines, make a foundation of weight and dignity.

The horizontal line is as quiet and placid as the vertical line is strong. It is the line of the great, flat expanses—the deserts, the prairies, calm lakes, and remote mountain ranges. It is the far-distant horizon where the earth and the sky come to rest. In Plate 5 the plant material is strong, even wiry; yet the whole effect is peaceful because of the low, wide spread of the lines. The short, diagonal upthrusts of the flax leaves give body and support to the basic horizontal but in no way detract from its serenity. Such an arrangement looks best on a low table.

The curved line suggests the fullness and the roundness of creature comforts and of home, as well as the perfection and the completeness of eternity. In Plate 6 the single flower at rest in its circle of leaves is suited to any low, flat surface. The broken circle of leaves is far more effective than an entire round of radiating lines. The variation introduced by the folded leaves is exactly right to represent the desire of a curved line to return to its source.

One of the problems that arise to distress the floral artist is the difficulty of securing a pronounced three-dimensional effect. Most arrangements are intended to be seen from only one point of view. The easy thing, then, is to dispose the material in a manner that will make a lovely front-view spread in one plane. But if you are not careful, you will produce the illusion of a cut-out. Working from front to back, setting your placements not

PLATE 3

Arrangements with religious connotations should be beautiful but simple. One branch of pear blossom was selected because of the unusual circumstance of three vertical growths springing from the same branch. The lowest placement is another branch of the same material. The lilies have been set to repeat the lines of the main placement. The simplicity of the white vase and the figure of St. Francis beside it complete a design that is as reverential as it is lovely.

14

PLATE 4

Here are two sprays of dried genista, the taller of them bent to assume a slight curve while it was still fresh. Careful pruning eliminated enough of the material to create interesting voids in the pattern, for natural genista is somewhat disordered. The central placement of driftwood was selected because its serrations resemble the lines of the genista and the Chinese tomb figurines. Heads of dried yarrow supply a bit of bright color for a pattern that so largely is made up of green, brown, and gray.

PLATE 5

Low tables require an arrangement that is beautiful when viewed from above. A silhouetted pattern is desirable for such locations because it does not take much material. The horizontal wooden container holds two opening bud stalks of New Zealand flax inserted in a pin-type holder and bent down at their stem bases to lean out horizontally. Buds and blossom of the cup of gold low in the center of the design furnish the accent.

16

PLATE 6

The hydrangea is the subject of this arrangement. Even the common, most ordinary hydrangea is a lovely flower; but this choice specimen is a hybrid of unusually delicate pink, whose foliage is ivory tinged with green. The exact spacing of the tips of the leaves, together with the intricate pattern of the venation, give the background far more importance to the design than most circular arrangements show. The material is set far back in the large plate used for container, the pin-type holder concealed by a narrow row of furled leaves. This position uses the water in the foreground as a part of the design.

17

parallel but in carefully chosen angles, you will produce a series of recessive planes that, when properly filled out, will show the rounded contours of complete form (Plate 7).

All surfaces have a definite textural quality. Often it is more easily perceived through touch than through sight because of the make-up of the surface—slick, rough, hairy, prickly. Texture is not so important to the arrangement as the other elements, though sometimes you work for textural unity (Plate 8) or textural contrast (Plate 9). But texture is so easily modified by other plant characteristics that it is sometimes difficult to analyze. Consider, for example, the petals of the Iceland poppy and some of the tuberous begonias. Though they are similar in the extreme satin shine of the surface, that likeness is not so apparent as the likeness of hue. The difference in the shape of the blossoms directs attention to the general appearance of the flowers rather than to any one fine detail; and general appearance is always more revealing of color than of texture. One corolla is cup-shaped, the other is flat; one has single petals, the other is overlapped in double structure; one is paper-thin, the other is thicker, heavier. These qualities are not textural, but they affect our interpretation of texture.

The pattern of the arrangement is made up of the lines, masses, planes, and spaces set in accordance with a plan. The empty spaces, or voids, are important features in the design. They function as a means of isolation, to single out plant material of particular significance, and as a device for rhythmic movement through the design (Plate 10). Voids figure more prominently in contemporary design than in the arrangements of thirty years ago, because open designs are more suitable for placement in the broad areas of the modern home than closely packed compositions. Ordinarily the pattern is a geometric form; that is, its contours suggest the peripheral lines of a triangle (Plate 11), a curve (Plate 12), or some other shape. There is a reason for this. Triangles and curves are known forms; they are easily recognized. An abundance of color in the arrangement will not confuse the observer, nor cause him to lose sight of the whole picture, if the colorful material is set in a familiar shape. The form must be familiar, but the presentation must not be entirely familiar. The triangle is centuries old; the artist must stamp it with his own personality, his individuality. The change

PLATE 7

To many people the valley lily and the camellia are choice blooms. The valley lily grows abundantly in a limited area of the United States, and the camellia has been so extensively cultivated that only the newer hybrids provoke much comment. Because of the lavish growth of both flowers their inherent beauty is all too frequently overlooked. Both of them are texturally exquisite. They differ completely in form and manner of growth, two qualities often considered desirable in a combination. This arrangement shows the success with which disparate materials can be combined.

PLATE 8

This tight little pattern is intended for a centerpiece for a luncheon. It is, of course, entirely impractical for a conventional dining-table arrangement, but it does exemplify some of the characteristics of centerpiece design. The balance with which the bunches of dark purple violets and the round clusters of pink dombeya have been placed suggests the symmetry of table arrangement; the beauty of the glass container is remindful of the crystal and the glass service. Since the conical composition has been made by a simple piling of each bunch on those below, it can be easily disassembled at the conclusion of the meal to present each guest with a boutonniere.

PLATE 9

When only one design is set on a mantel, it usually is symmetrical. Although the pattern of the formal triangle is stylized, interesting variation within the framework is highly desirable. The bells of Ireland on the left combine with the aspidistra on the right to form a second triangle. Geranium leaves repeat the same shape for center placement. The repetition establishes a strong feeling of rhythm.

21

PLATE 10

The Japanese plum is perhaps the earliest of the fruit trees to blossom. In regions with mild winters the dombeya is in flower at the same time as the plum. In this design they are combined. The color pattern is very delicate; it is indicative of the pale hues of the early spring blossoms. Blush pink of the plum blossoms almost conceals the brown stems, so profuse is the floral growth. The powder pink of the dombeya at the base rests against the soft pink lining of the container. The outer surface of the bowl is brown like the branch of the plum.

PLATE 11

An urn of classic simplicity is fit container for a symmetrical design of choice material. In this composition three sprays of white stock establish the tallest vertical placement supported by spires of lavender Canterbury bells. Some of the bells strengthen the center of the pattern and others make the basal lines of the triangle. White blossoms of beaumontia in the center form a small triangle from whose points branches of white ivy leaves run diagonally through the composition.

PLATE 12

 Two black glass plates are placed side by side, their dark-rimmed outlines suggesting a figure 8. A garland of grapes, with leaves and tendrils, is the only means of decoration. The simplicity of the design is satisfying.

24

probably is slight, but even a small deviation can be a mark of originality. Plate 13 is a modified Georgian design. It is sufficiently Georgian in its principles to justify its inclusion in the chapter on period arrangements. But it is not entirely Georgian. Had it been true to its models, the voids would have been filled with the large leaf forms that the Georgians delighted to use. It would have been a full package of plant material. So designed, it would have been highly appropriate for museum placement, like most truly traditional arrangements. The variations—the liberties, if you please—planned by the artist have kept it recognizable as Georgian in spirit, but have made it highly attractive for the contemporary home. The arranger remained strictly within the confines of his pattern, but he ranged freely; and, by so doing, he stamped the arrangement with his own personality.

The last point to note about pattern is the necessity for maintaining some standard of proportion or scale. Size is purely relative. A vase with its complement of flowers which seems right in one setting may be dwarfed to insignificance in a second location, or toweringly huge in a third place, all within the same house. It is a matter of arrangement against background in an environment. A design must be prepared for a particular position.

The last important element of design, color, is so vital to the floral artist that it has been given special treatment in a separate chapter.

There are many occasions when an artist prefers an Oriental type of design to the more familiar Western arrangement. Ikebana, or the Japanese art of arranging plant material, has several types or schools. The oldest and most rigidly classical, the Rikkwa style, is too large and formal for our taste; we can enjoy the Shōkwa and the Moribana styles. The formal Shōkwa design is always upright. Like all true Japanese compositions, it consists of three principal placements representing heaven, man, and earth, all of which must be curved, though perhaps only slightly. The main line, *shin* or heaven, is very tall, sometimes three or four times the height of the container. The curve of this line is complex. It must be very dexterously manipulated; and if the shaping is not skillfully done, the chief beauty of the design will be lost. The curve may not be fuller than the fattest

PLATE 13

An urn of rare glass is used for a design intended to suggest the Georgian period. This style requires a great deal of material. Lilies mottled in ruby red and blades of white cane grass make the longest placements. The center is filled with a mass of pale yellow star-of-Bethlehem clusters surrounded by roses, carnations, and chrysanthemums. Georgian arrangements call for a closely packed bouquet. This modification is more pleasing to modern taste than an accurate reproduction of the eighteenth-century style.

portion of the container; the point of return must bring the top directly above the place where *shin* emerged from the water. The man line, *soe*, is about two thirds as tall as *shin*. It may curve to the right or the left of *shin* and consequently may extend beyond the widest circumference of the vase. *Tai*, the earth line, is the shortest, approximately half the length of *soe*. It is placed, and it curves, in a reverse direction to the position taken by *soe*. The stems of the placements must be so close together that they seem to be one stalk, and this tree trunk effect must be maintained for at least three inches above the water. Usually the artist includes more than three branches of material, but any additional placements are added as complements to these three main stems, as if they were branches. To maintain the proper slenderness of the pattern the artist uses material that can be manipulated freely and that will hold the induced curves. The semiformal and the informal styles of Shōkwa design permit a broader lateral curve than is seen in the formal Shōkwa; the *soe* and the *tai* placements extend much farther outside the container (Plate 14).

Moribana is the type of design evolved early in the twentieth century under the impact of Western civilization. The influence of the Shōkwa style is apparent together with a definite freshness, and some of the feeling of the Western bouquet with its pronounced three-dimensional form. Since the word *moribana* means "piles of flowers arranged in a bowl," the name would seem to indicate a lavish use of flowers in a rather formless pattern. The designer must not be misled; the Japanese pattern of three main levels is still present, though not so obviously as in the Shōkwa design. These Moribana placements, called *ichi, ni,* and *san,* are comparable to the heaven, man, and earth lines of the classic school; but their lengths have not the rigid mathematical proportions of the Shōkwa designs. The intent of Moribana is to indicate naturalistic growth or landscape effects; and since the artist may use any number of placements to imply a landscape idea, with its foreground scenery and remote distance, the composition will have a pronounced feeling of depth (Plate 15). One of the greatest difficulties the American designer encounters with Moribana designs is to represent the natural growth of his plants. To do that, he must understand their growth at all seasons. The home gardener who selects his

PLATE 14

The apple tree was carefully studied for suitable subject matter before this branch was cut. It establishes the two levels of the informal Japanese pattern. The third level is made by a camellia branch. The upper compartment of the bamboo stalk holds a single cutting of azalea.

28

PLATE 15

The Japanese realistic style of arrangement results in designs of great simplicity. Such a pattern must interpret the natural growth of a plant, and it must exhibit the three levels of Japanese taste. The clivia of this arrangement is presented from the unopened bud through full bloom and seed capsule. The large container is in earth tones, and the damp wood suggests the shady coolness of the environment that the clivia requires.

material from the border over which he has toiled all year will understand the behavioristic alterations in appearance of his plants and will know precisely how to represent spring, summer, and winter (Plate 16).

Design, Occidental or Oriental, is age-old. Many generations are required for a pattern cycle. The formulation of a new pattern, the displaying of a new style, is done by bold thinkers, defiant of custom and heedless of criticism. There are two notes of possible originality today. Designers of unusual creative ability are making lavish use of foliage material rather than flowers, and they are devising startling compositions through the development of abstract patterns. Whether either of these will win sufficient popular approval to develop into a general style is as yet unknown.

PLATE 16

A delicate pattern, fresh and cool as early spring, has been built on a flagstone base. Two stalks of Easter lilies stand above a footing of azaleas, as they may have grown in the garden border. Fronds of maidenhair and an earth cover of baby-tears conceal the pin-type holder and, at the same time, intensify the illusion of border planting.

31

CHAPTER III

Color

COLOR IS most beautiful. All people have loved it. In the ancient world of the Mediterranean the purple dye of the Phoenicians was priced in terms of a king's ransom. Yet monarchs used it freely. Cleopatra visited Mark Antony in a ship whose stern was beaten gold, whose tackle was silken, whose sails were purple. The reds of the Chinese, the rich hues of the Byzantine mosaics, the clear blue that the artists of the Renaissance reserved for the robe of the Virgin—across the world from the Orient to the West and down to our own time the best craftsmen of the ages have applied their skill to the service of color. When Juliana of the House of Orange, heir to the throne of the Netherlands, reached her majority, her countrymen created for her a vase of pure beauty. It is molded glass of simple line and limpid clearness, orange in shape, ripe orange in color—glass that glows with mellow fire as one turns it in the hand.

Color is used so freely in home decoration that the establishment of color has been the average homemaker's main purpose in setting flowers within the house. Modern gardens afford a riot of color. The American landscape, for instance, planted generously with native bloom and domesticated exotics, is bright in the heat of summer and the cold of winter. Of course, the inexperienced arranger chooses colors with abandon because of their eye-catching qualities.

That colors discreetly combined in subtle harmonies are more satisfying than flamboyant display is a lesson that has to be learned. You will find that the lesson is time-consuming. You must master a brief vocabulary. Early in this schooling process you discover there are six plainly evident spectrum colors that may be distinguished in any completely formed rainbow: red, orange, yellow, green, blue, and violet. If the rainbow lasts long enough, you can see that the colors are not sharply separated in knife-edge bands, but that each one imperceptibly shades off and blends into the next color. Between any two colors of the rainbow are others made of this blending. Those which can be discerned are named for their two adjacent neighbors, as red-orange, yellow-green, and blue-violet. Three of the six principal colors—red, yellow, and blue—are said to be primary, because when mixed in a beam of light they make white light. If the red, yellow, and blue are pigments, the mixture will be black paint. The other three colors—orange, green, and violet—are called secondary, because each one is an admixture of the two primaries between which it stands. The six spectrum colors, together with their blends, form the color wheel: red, red-orange, orange, yellow-orange, yellow, yellow-green, green, blue-green, blue, blue-violet, violet, red-violet and back again to red.

As you continue your study of vocabulary, you learn that each of these colors is properly called a hue. Blue-green, then, is a hue. Not all blue-greens are equally intense. If the hue has all the color that can possibly be poured into it, like a saturate solution, so that it is full strength, it is of strong chroma. Chroma, therefore, is the strength or the weakness of the hue. Again, not all blue-greens are equally dark or light. Each of the blue-greens may have the same blending of blue and green; but the light blue-greens show a mixing with white, and the dark blue-greens a mixing with black. The result is said to be the value of the hue. Spectrum colors mixed with white to produce light values are sometimes called tints of those colors; mixed with black to produce dark values, they are called shades. If gray has been mixed with the blue-green, the hue is said to have been changed in tone.

To summarize now:

HUE is the name of the color.

CHROMA indicates the intensity.

VALUE measures the darkness or the lightness in TINTS or SHADES.

TONE indicates a graying of the hue.

Black, white, and gray are called NEUTRALS.

Red, orange, and yellow are the warm colors. They are strong and bold and dramatic. They are rich and stimulating.

Blue, green, and violet are the cool colors of peace and repose. Quiet and restrained, they suggest calm and rest.

Before proceeding further, if you are a beginner in flower arrangement, you may well take time to reflect. You should apply to your understanding of color terms the basic facts about the colors of flowers which you have learned from your garden. You know, for one thing, that flowers apparently change in color from early morning to late afternoon and that, when picked, they frequently do not seem to be of entirely the same color as before cutting.

In your border planting you have discovered that the color of flowers is affected by the kind of foliage against which they are planted. Blossoms that glowed brilliantly against a dark green shrub may seem paler, gray-washed, if transplanted to the vicinity of a light-colored foliage plant. Other flowers appear most vivid when set among plants with leaves of silver-gray. You remember, also, your experience in the border with the effect of light. Warm-colored flowers, especially those in any portion of the orange segment of the color wheel, are intensified in hue during that part of the day when they are in direct sunlight, but immediately appear darker, or at least duller, if clouds slip over the sun. Contrariwise, in the same exposure your blue and violet blossoms seem lighter in value in bright sunlight, but maintain their original intensity when the shadows cover them. These same effects will be apparent in an arrangement. To maintain any particular brilliance of hue, then, you must combine your blossoms with the same consideration that you exercised in planting them; and, after arrangement, you must place them in a location suitably lighted, else you may lose the effect you desired in hue, value, and chroma.

As a beginning arranger, you will notice that the same color combinations that are attractive in the border will be pleasing in an arrangement. If you prefer closely related colors, you may wish to try a monochromatic design; that is, a pattern worked out in a single hue, any one of the twelve segments of the wheel (Plate 17). To have "a single hue" does not mean that you must use only flowers cut from one bush to maintain complete identity of color. You may use flowers of light and dark values

PLATE 17

Long cuttings of foliage geranium, variegated green and white, have been placed in a white container to make the tallest and the lowest placements. The curves at the tip ends are natural. White azaleas form the center of the design. The completed arrangement has been set on a stand painted green for St. Patrick's Day.

of your chosen color, both tints and shades; you may range into the grayed tones. After you have exhausted the possibility of color, you will spice your arrangement by the use of differing flower forms: spike flowers and disk flowers, preferably blossoms that vary in texture and size. A monochromatic arrangement can be quiet and calm. Placed in a room decorated in crnately patterned furnishings, it may serve as a center of interest for tired eyes.

When you begin to assemble hues for a floral design, you discover that, like dear and lasting friendships, the most pleasing harmonies are made up of either closely related colors or colors that demonstrate the attraction of opposites. A closely related color harmony is called analogous (Plate 18). It consists of one hue supplemented by adjacent hues. The color dominating the harmony will be any one of the twelve segments of the wheel. The other members of the harmony may be the hues standing on either or both sides of the dominant color. In a strictly technical sense, you can effect an analogy through the use of two colors. Such a color pattern may not satisfy, however. With a combination of three colors you can skillfully blend your hues. Through the use of these transitions you avoid spottiness; therefore you secure such rhythm that the eye moves easily through the pattern. Should a third color not be possible in flowers, it can be introduced in the container. The color of the container is always one of the hues chosen for the composition. In a technical sense, again, the analogy, like the monochrome, may introduce all values and intensities of the harmony; but in practice it is most successful to maintain a closeness of both value and intensity. This precaution will prevent spottiness. It is all too easy for tints to pass unnoticed in a design constructed largely of deep tones. For purposes of emphasis a rich shade may be used as center of interest in an arrangement of light colors, where the small placement of dark color will balance the much larger amount of light color (Plate 19).

The other type of harmony, the arrangement of opposites, is the complementary harmony (Plate 20). A separation of hues as wide apart as blue and orange, or violet and yellow, or yellow-green and red-violet, suggests the shock of violence. The effect is, of course, very dynamic and exceedingly dramatic. As

PLATE 18

This composition in analogous harmony uses odds and ends of garden supply. The delicate lace of the bamboo is in the lightest tint of yellow-green. Three spikes of yellow gladiolus and two blossoming spikes of yellow-orange canna rise from the base against the background of bamboo. The container is an unusual piece of crackleware in yellow-green with a rough, black lava glaze.

37

PLATE 19

Another arrangement in analogous color harmony has been developed in cool tones. Centered is a bunch of violets outlined with heads of lavender allium. Long racemes of orchid lilac complete the floral pattern. The container is Wedgwood blue.

38

PLATE 20

    Six leaves of aspidistra have been arranged in a pattern that can function alone as a foliage composition. By covering the flowers, you can discover the charm of the green design. The two blossoms are pink peonies, and the container is pink.

with all extremes, it can easily be overdone. That is one of the reasons why the conventional Christmas decoration of red and green is gradually being supplanted, or at least supplemented, by a more subtle combination: blue with silver, or silver-gray with frosty green. Unless you intend your complementary harmony to evoke surprise along with appreciation, you will tie the arrangement into its setting. Perhaps one of the hues of the harmony repeats a hue used in the room decoration; or perhaps you have placed near the vase an accessory to echo its tone. The analogous harmony may concern itself with any segment of the color wheel, but the complementary is restricted. The least garish effects, and therefore the most pleasing, are secured through the use of yellow and violet, blue and orange.

Variations of the complementary scheme often more successful than the pure complementary, because less violent, are the near-complementary and the split-complementary. The near-complementary uses two colors: the selected hue and the hue neighboring its complement, instead of the complement itself. If, then, violet is chosen as the dominant hue, the other member of the harmony will be yellow-green or yellow-orange instead of yellow. The shock of the direct complement is subtly modified by the delicate intrusion of a third color; because, though neither green nor orange is actually present, the hue is felt along with the yellow of the blends (Plate 21).

The split-complementary uses three actual colors, the dominant hue together with the two neighbors of the complement (Plate 22). In this harmony, through the use of violet with yellow-green and yellow-orange, you feel the presence of four hues, with effortless transitions throughout the design. Pastels are more successful than dark shades for this type of arrangement.

The last type of color harmony is the triad (Plate 23). The success of this combination is due to the old truth that a whole is usually more satisfying than any of its parts. A triad is a combination of three hues through whose movement the design completes the color wheel. Whether you employ the primaries, the secondaries, or the blends, you select a hue from each of the three main sections of the wheel to tip the points of your equilateral triangle: red, yellow, and blue; orange, green, and violet; yellow-orange, blue-green, and red-violet; yellow-

PLATE 21

This arrangement exemplifies the near-complementary color harmony. In a deep purple bowl two eggplants have been impaled on sticks. Yellow-green peas and peppers provide textural harmony. To make the rosette effects, the artist wired the stem ends of the peas in clusters. The violet cabbage gives textural contrast, and its heavy venation provides an additional interest.

PLATE 22

This whimsical Easter design is a split-complementary color harmony. Little white eggcups are the containers for the miniature arrangement. Valley lilies make the tallest placement, their tiny white bells shining clearly against the pronounced yellow-green of their foliage. Apricot roses and apricot azaleas with small bunches of violets complete the color detail.

PLATE 23

The principle of the triad in color harmony is worked out in this informal placement for a mantel. Yellow-green aspidistra leaves make a permanent framework that can be filled, if you wish, with any available flowers. Kniphofia blossoms in red-orange are used here. Three leaves of tree cineraria complete the base of the arrangement in the blue-violet bowl. The pheasants are of Venetian glass, blue-violet mottled with yellow-green and red-orange. The mantel is correctly decorated with a floral piece set off-center and balanced by accessories to give the feeling of symmetry.

green, blue-violet, and red-orange. Any one of these combinations supplies an abundance of color interest, at the same time providing smooth transitions within the design. While the hues are widely separated, they lack the sharp contrast, the possible dissonance, of the direct complement. And they are more lively than the analogous harmony.

CHAPTER IV

The Beauty of Foliage

SOME OF THE most interesting developments in floral design have been initiated and worked out by amateurs. One of these contributions, and probably the most valuable, is the use of foliage either alone or in combination with flowers.

The commercial man has always relied on the standard material of ferns, galax leaves, and a few other kinds of greenery. But he has limited their use to so-called fillers. He has not built his compositions to dramatize the beauty of green leaves. The amateur can show him the way to that expertness. By means of trial and struggle the amateur discovered the loveliness of form and texture in leaf and bough. His acute awareness of color values taught him the great range of greens in different leaves. Through the plainness of leafage he learned how to perfect the severe beauty of simple lines. Today foliage is one of the greatest assets of the floral artist. It becomes the background against which flowers are dramatized (Plates 24, 25). It may, as well, be used alone; for it offers as many contrasts in color and form as do flowers themselves (Plate 26).

As a plant grower you have learned to see shades of green, gray, red, and bronze in your foliage. You grow it for the permanent beauty it gives your garden. But you find that as cut material it lasts almost as long within the house as on the plant.

Sprays and large branches of such evergreen material as magnolia, lemon leaves, camellia, huckleberry, and rhododendron have long been commonplace decorations in homes and public buildings. They are cool and clean; they fill a large space acceptably; they do not need to be fussed over. As huge green bouquets set in tall containers, even without any particular

PLATE 24

    Bearded iris shows the beauty of complete simplicity. The arrangement of the leaves, set in groups of three, gives rhythmic movement through the pointed tips and the folded loops. One specimen flower with its bud provides the color accent. The container is a vertical cylinder of bamboo with a tiny spray of its own growth still apparent.

46

PLATE 25

The plants of this arrangement are unusually choice. Ivy is a very common vine, but the leaves of this ivy are distinctive in shape and color: thin almost to sheerness and white, as if carved from ivory. The single blossom of epiphyllum, deep cream with a throat of lime green, is virtually luminous, so rich is the sheen of its petals. The container is a shell with color shadings from ivory to pink.

PLATE 26

A *pattern in complementary harmony has been worked out with foliage. Leaves of the Rex begonia are green with white flecks. The ornamental geranium leaves are burgundy through red-brown. The ceramic container is green. The shape and the coloring of the foliage make it appear more like flower forms than plant leaves. This arrangement is an example of the extreme versatility of foliage for purposes of design.*

attempt at arrangement, they possess an undeniable charm. But their strong lines offer almost unlimited possibilities for dramatic treatment. Arranged primarily for lineal beauty, they can be patterned after the Japanese classical style (Plate 27), or in the less stylized manner of the Japanese naturalistic portrayal (Plate 28). The clean-cut edges of blade and leaf appeal through their precision; they suggest a beauty not readily achieved with flower forms. Their definite contours guide you to fresh designs in keeping with modern ideals of simplicity (Plates 29, 30).

Leaves display many attributes of loveliness. Their textures are even more varied than the textures of blossoms. For compositions of strong lines you may choose leaves that are leathery to the touch. Some of these have a surface of high gloss. Most extreme is the coprosma, because of its brilliance called the looking-glass plant. Others with high sheen are the camellia, the magnolia, the rubber plant, clivia, ivy, and aspidistra. Some have a soft sheen; they display almost a diffused glow, such as the viburnum, the rhododendron, the lemon, the aralia, and New Zealand flax. Others of scant sheen are the eucalyptus, the sea grape, and the bird of paradise. The tough surface of these leaves makes them easy to manipulate, and their firmness ensures a stability of position in the pattern. Or you may prefer blades that are soft as suede or velour. If you need high brilliance, use the elaeagnus or the African silver tree. The cecropia is more subdued. The dusty miller, the dombeya, and the globe artichoke have almost no sheen to brighten their softness.

Of equal interest with the range in textural characteristics is the diversity in shape. Most of the leaves in your garden are single blades with a smooth or serrate edge. The azalea and the camellia have this simple form. The leaves of your roses are compound, for several blades grow from one stalk. These leaves are small, compact, and relatively inconspicuous. Long, narrow leaves make good vertical placements in your design, especially those with some specific quality of beauty. The thin cylinders of the equisetum are more arresting in their delicacy than many larger forms because of their ridges and bands. Strap leaves of the clivia and the agapanthus show the slightest of softened curves that combine smartly with the star shapes of the aloe and other succulents. You have disk shapes, also, in the

PLATE 27

The traditions of the Japanese classical school have been followed in this composition. Sprays of Japanese yew precisely set are
displayed in a bronze container of Japanese origin. A primitive Y-
shaped holder secures the stems in a central grouping simulating the
trunk of a tree.

50

PLATE 28

A design of nandina and daisies is a realistic pattern, arranged after the natural manner of growth. The three stalks of nandina spread their foliage to the light with room at the base for the small cluster of daisies chosen for their several stages of flower development—from tightly closed bud to fully opened blossom. The composition is correctly proportioned to indicate relative size of the two plants. A cup pin-type holder is concealed by a fragment of tree root.

PLATE 29

    *This arrangement, really a variation of the design in Plate 2,
shows how the manner of manipulation can create a completely different feeling, though using materials and pattern that are very similar.
The blades are iris leaves of two varieties: the Siberian and the bearded.
Here the alternation of ascent from left to right is by groups rather
than by single leaves. The natural curve of the leaves breaks the pure
severity of the vertical column by providing an almost pendulant movement. The container is black lacquer, delicately thin as the leaf blades.*

PLATE 30

The rubber tree furnishes the material for this study in complementary color harmony. Seven of the highly glossy leaves have been
folded to show the blue-green coloring of the back of the leaf which
contrasts interestingly with the deep green of the surface gloss. Four
branch ends defoliated of all leaves crown the top of the folded-leaf
pattern. The red sheathing that encloses the tightly furled leaf buds
completes the color harmony.

53

echeveria and some foliage geraniums (Plate 9). Your pittos-porum leaves probably are whorled; that is, several leaf stalks are inserted at one point on the stem and grow in circles at the twig ends. These rounding pads of leaves are as suitable as any ray flower for design. In the spring and summer you look for foliage that is dainty rather than dramatic. Select a leaf that is twice or thrice compound—for instance, many ferns, plants of the carrot family, the acacias, and the jacaranda. Among the small flowering plants of the early garden the leaves of the columbine, the bleeding heart, and the thalictrums have the fragility of fine lace. Many of the bamboos display a handsome, feathery foliage (Plate 31). You will also need leaves that sug-gest power along with their beauty. The large leaves that you choose for accent placements are elegant because of the in-dividuality of their form: the dombeya leaf, sharply angled on the margin; the acanthus and the fig leaves with their deep, irregular lobes (Plate 32); the leaf of the castor bean, divided nearly to the middle; and the cut-leaf philodendron with its deep voids.

Leaf detail can be as interesting as the entire form. Conspic-uous venation invariably attracts attention. It is always arranged in a design, it frequently adds an additional factor to the color pattern of the leaf, and it invites the pleasure of touch as you trace the intricacies of its network with your fingertip. Since the veins are usually raised on the back of the leaf, and there-fore more prominent than on the face, you will discover that to place some leaves facing front, others reversed, will provide an additional means of variation in your pattern.

The beauty of texture and shape in foliage patterns tempts the arranger to endless effort, even without the fascination of color. Yet almost every hue, together with its tints and its shades, is apparent to the trained eye. The greens predominate, but in the vegetation of our green world there is no monotony. Beautiful blue-greens of the Colorado spruce and the eucalyptus offer rest and comfort to tired eyes. For that reason they are often planted at the back of deep lawns or gardens to increase the feeling of distance. The yellow-greens in the bamboo delight us with their frivolous gaiety.

Many of the unusual color effects stem from variegation or combination. The yellow-leaved privet and the yellow-flecked

PLATE 31

One spray of miniature bamboo was severely pruned for two reasons. The more important of the two aims was to make a delicate, lacelike pattern for the erect placement. The second purpose was to provide short wisps of leaves and stems which could be assembled in bundles and set in a tufted mound to cover a pin-type holder. Extreme defoliation, such as was given this branch, followed by complete immersion for first conditioning, will keep the bamboo crisp and fresh for days. The Chinese basket woven of reeds is a fitting container for this Oriental plant.

PLATE 32

Most blade leaves are thin and so flat that a leaf arrangement is likely to lose the effect of depth necessary to a well-planned design. Careful manipulation of the foliage can correct this tendency. Here six leaves of ginger have been folded at the midrib, then set in a pin-type holder so that they overlap in receding planes. Three aralia leaves for basal placement, one behind the other, bring the design completely to the front and over the edge of the container. Thus an unquestionable third-dimensional feeling has been secured.

aucuba are examples of nature's dramatic color harmonies (Plate 33). The white-bladed cane grass and the spectacular green-and-white-striped banana leaf or aspidistra, the partially white hosta and the white and green or all-white ivy, the mottled dieffenbachia and the elaborately patterned caladium, owe their extravagant beauty to nature's fastidious taste in color combinations.

The narrow, overlapping leaves of the rhoeo build mellow piles of royal purple. Trimmings of violet and red-violet enrich the maranta leaves and those of the coleus and the cabbage. Large splotches of intense red-violet on the leaves of the majestic Sumatra banana are as vivid as though artificially painted.

The coleus grown in cooler climates and the dracaena and the caladium of the greenhouse or the more temperate regions display a full range of color from tints of pink through ruby red to burnished rust. All gardeners know the Japanese plum and some kinds of barberry and canna that reach from rich burgundy tones through the scale of muted reds and bronze. Exotic plants have even more remarkable color patterns, like the variety of heliconia which is texturally slick as highly polished leather—it is fantastically unreal with its tan-colored leaves. The brown dapplings on the pitcher plant of our own swamps appear as artificially contrived as the brown variegation in the leaf of the ornamental foliage geranium (Plate 26). These colorings are extreme, particularly in the richness of their dark tones; but you can find even deeper hues. It does not seem possible that vegetation can be black. Yet in some kinds are shades so dark that the ordinary observer will name them black without question: in croton leaves, vividly spotted with a blaze of strong yellow and fiery orange; and in the rhubarb chard, black-leaved with bright red or orange midrib.

The leaves of many plants maintain a constant color quality. From the first unfurled bud of spring to late autumn growth they display an unvarying color. But the new growth of shrubs such as the eugenia and the nandina is a moist, warm red that changes to the green of maturity. Throughout the growing season their green-leaved branches are tipped with red-leaved twigs.

Consider next the color mutations due to seasonal change or the effect of soil constituents, and color variations caused by

PLATE 33

The diagonal is a forceful and dramatic line implying the intent or the performance of rapid action. It is always strong and vivid. Two long leaves of aspidistra establish the dominant line, with two more leaves parallel to reinforce and extend the basic plane. Seven leaves of aucuba provide color interest through their yellow-spotted green surfaces.

control of moisture and sunlight. For example, the bells of Ireland when grown in semi-shade are a deep blue-green; when planted in full sun, they mature just as completely, but the color of the plants is a crisp yellow-green or emerald green. Aspidistra in poor soil will be striped white, cream, or pale yellow and is frequently called the variegated aspidistra. These stripes disappear if the plant is set in a rich soil. Color value within a plant can be controlled by its environment, even if very slightly. It is this subtlety of color which gives to foliage arrangements a quiet distinction infrequently achieved by the designer working in floral color (Plate 34).

Aside from the aesthetic values of foliage, some practical qualities found in leafage but not in flowers are worthy of consideration. The long life of a foliage design is of major significance. Branches of evergreen trees, particularly the conifers, last for months or even a year. The large bamboo when properly treated will last a year and continue to supply new leaf growth. Cut aspidistra leaves remain fresh for two months or more, dracaena likewise. English ivy will root and grow when shaped into the trailing arrangements suited to vines (Plate 35). The succulents, such as the aloe and echeveria, and the cut leaves of the sansevieria also contribute durability to design. Experimentation will give you all the information you need. You will discover so many plants with lasting qualities that you will never lack material of this kind.

Another advantage of foliage is that it does not absorb water so rapidly as cut flowers; therefore the chore of adding water frequently is eliminated. For the busy housewife time is an important factor in the maintenance of floral décor. The increasing use of dried arrangements has been the result of this desire for more free time and a release from the necessity of continually working with cut flowers. Dried arrangements are appropriate in some settings, but in the vast majority of homes designs of living foliage are more suitable.

CARE AND TREATMENT

The preparation of cut foliage and branch materials for arrangements is a very simple process. Strip all basal foliage from the main stalk that is to be immersed in water. Two thirds of the

PLATE 34

Two Japanese containers of driftwood have been placed one atop the other and slightly askew. Four aspidistra leaves, turned to form a patterned vertical, are balanced by the single leaf that leans from the container at the bottom to provide a base line strong enough to support the height of the off-center vertical. The color pattern is severely simple. The containers are gray and black; the leaves are striped white and green; the tiny figure of the woman with her water bucket is black, white, and gray.

PLATE 35

Ivy is one of the most durable of evergreen materials. Arranged in water, it will root and grow, lasting for many months. Two varieties of ivy compose this twin mantel arrangement. The long sprays are of the miniature-leaved ivy; at the center is a rosette effect with leaves of the larger English ivy. The arrangement on the right, vivid with dark red cherries, shows how effectively fruit or flowers may be added to an all-green composition.

61

stem of the average garden flower is defoliated before immersion, but four or five inches is sufficient for foliage. Because the stem end of some branches is very tough, you must make several vertical cuts in the end of the stalk. These slashes encourage a free flow of water and at the same time make the blunt end easier to impale on a needlepoint holder. After cleaning—and very little is required with foliage, since most kinds are slick and smooth, such as the aspidistra, the iris, or the bird-of-paradise leaf—immerse the plant materials at least two thirds of their length for a short time only. This immersion forces a free flow of water, and as soon as the vegetation appears to be crisp, it is ready for arrangement. The depth of the water is comparatively unimportant with most foliage since it will last in shallow water. If, then, the design and the location require a low bowl, the condition of the arrangement will not be impaired.

Some foliage, particularly the broad-bladed varieties, such as the canna, the banana, the caladium, the dieffenbachia, and the castor bean, requires complete immersion after the stem has been cleaned. When crisp to the touch, regardless of the minutes or hours spent in this bath, the materials are ready for arranging.

All cactus growths, succulents, and the cut blades of sansevieria, and similar fibrous types, along with the agave and the century plant, must be kept dry. They are not to be conditioned in water, nor placed in water after being arranged. They last for months when not in water.

PRINCIPLES OF DESIGN

In making a design of foliage alone, follow the same principles of composition which are applied to floral art. In a vertical arrangement you will substitute tall leaves for the spiked floral forms to establish the lines (Plate 2). In a formal triangular plan for the distribution of the material, place the vertical lines of foliage in the upright central position and horizontal placements extending equidistant. Complete the design with clusters of leaves centered in rosette fashion at the axis in the same manner that a disk-type blossom would be used within a triangular framework of spiked floral forms (Plate 36).

Foliage makes a superior design in the informal triangular pattern. Few flower forms assume the soft, curved arc so neces-

PLATE 36

The lines of this formal triangle are established by green canna leaves. The blades of the vertical placements are set with some of them facing the observer, others reversed to show the contrast of venation. Two long leaves of equal length make the lowest horizontal lines. Other leaves, shortened and creased, support the horizontal lines and fill the space to meet the vertical placement. One magnolia tip whose leaves form a rosette conceals the meeting of the vertical and the horizontal lines. Three tightly furled magnolia buds add an interesting diagonal to this foliage design.

sary for the establishment of the primary tallest line. The curved branch provided naturally on shrubs has no floral substitute (Plate 37).

Should you wish a radiating line, one upright rounded leaf or palm frond establishes the form. A meticulous placing of many stalks of larkspur or other tall flower forms would be required to secure a similar effect.

COLOR HARMONIES

Color is a stable instrument. The same principles of harmony prevail in working with foliage and in manipulating flowers, but finer discernment is necessary. Since green is the dominant hue, and sometimes the only hue, you must train your eye to determine true green, to recognize blue-green and yellow-green, and to differentiate between them; you must discriminate, eventually, between each of them and true green and thus set the three greens into separate classifications. This is frequently a difficult task, but once your eye is trained to be highly observant, the color problem will present no further difficulties. The true green of the aspidistra, combined with the yellow-green leaves of the aucuba with its pure yellow dapplings, make an analogous composition employing three colors: green, yellow-green, and yellow (Plate 33).

When the tightly furled new leaf buds of the rubber plant are used with the matured green leaves, the red envelope surrounding the bud makes a complementary harmony with the green leaves.

Quite startling color combinations are possible if you want a highly dramatic design. A composition using violet cabbage and small yellow-green Osage oranges makes a smart near-complementary harmony. The cabbage leaf can be set either as background or as encirclement for the fruit. The textural contrast between the sateen smoothness of the cabbage and the pebbled surface of the orange, together with the similarity of their rounded forms, create an exceedingly clever design from very simple material.

Foliage can also be used for artful monochromatic patterns. Since white, gray, and black are considered neutrals rather than colors, a design composed of the white and green aspidistra

PLATE 37

Two large branches of loquat were selected for the beauty of their leaves and their generous clusters of fruit. The tall placement was not artificially shaped; the curve is the natural manner of growth. Though the material seems casually set in the heavy, brown pottery container, the arrangement is far from aimless. For the lower branch at the right provides a successful balance to the heavy base of cryptomeria wood and also completes the triangular pattern of the branches. Another triangle is formed by the position of the vase on the wooden slab.

leaves in a white, gray, black, or green container of identical hue would be interpreted as monochromatic in green (Plate 34).

Perhaps you think of landscape growth in terms of tree and shrub. You would perhaps infer that a foliage arrangement would necessarily be built on a large scale commensurate with the size of tree or shrub. Realism does not go that far. A naturalistic design can be created appropriately from small cuttings taken from plants of large growth. By the manner of their manipulation any kind of desired effect can be built. Furthermore, large plant growths are in the minority in any ordinary landscape and especially so in any garden. You have only to look about you to see the great abundance of small growing things. A blade of grass, a frond of fern, an individual leaf, the tendril of a vine, all afford material for an arrangement composed on small scale to fit a definite purpose (Plate 35).

CONTAINERS

Just as flower forms determine the suitability of a container, so the nature of the foliage decides the vase to be used. Most foliage is purer in line than flowers, and quieter in color. Containers, therefore, should be simple, unadorned, and grayed rather than vivid in hue. The heaviness of the branch and the cumbersomeness of the stalk will determine both the size and the weight of the container. Landscape colors of green, brown, and gray are always suitable. The Japanese, experts in the arrangement of foliage, never permit emphasis on the receptacle, but subordinate it in quiet taste as contributing to the final beauty of the design.

PLANTERS

The appeal of flowers comes primarily from their prettiness, and floral designers use them in arrangements to enjoy that beauty. The Japanese have never used flowers in the Occidental manner simply for the loveliness of their decoration. Japanese designs use foliage expressive of seasonal and natural growth. When a flower is introduced it is not for purpose of accent, but because it belongs environmentally to the foliage in the arrangement (Plate 38). The Japanese garden from which that foliage has been taken is always small, always placed in an area related to the house, and always intended to be viewed as a part of the house. This relationship of house and garden is becoming established. In the United States, for instance, many homes now incorporate an enclosed garden as a feature of the home.

For those homes where interior plantings of this ambitious sort are not feasible, potted growth is a substitute. Once used solely for decorative purposes as floor placements at the entranceway or in living areas, potted plants were as conventionalized as the traditional umbrella stand and hat rack. Later fashion encouraged the use of potted ferns to be placed in a jardiniere, upright on stands or in window areas. Furniture makers even manufactured jardiniere stands in the nineteenth century with a hollow in the top into which the jardiniere could be lowered. The plant thus appeared to be sitting on the table. These effects were so happily received that the plantings were extended to include what might be termed typical house plants, such as the begonia and the geranium. The earlier use of large potted specimens for floor plants was primarily for decoration; the smaller plant was potted as a precautionary measure in an attempt to prolong its life—it was easy to carry indoors for protection against the harsh seasonal changes of cool climates and to move outside when the weather permitted.

This desire to have natural growth within the house has developed into a new horticultural expression. Extensive scientific research has taught us much about the habits of growth of common plants and the adaptability of the exotic novelties. New plant foods and fertilizers have been developed, along with a better understanding of soil composition. All of these factors have contributed to the brilliant success of this new art, the planter.

THE PLANTER CONTAINER

If you design your planter, you will be cautious in your selection of containers. You will discover that you are much more strictly limited than in your choice of vases. A life indoors

PLATE 38

Two branches of Japanese plum are set in naturalistic design in a heavy pottery container with the glossy front face of each leaf turned to the light. Green-throated primroses are clustered with their own foliage at the base of the tree, as if growing. The color pattern is mainly green, to echo the center of the primroses; for the plum branches range from green to brown, and the burnished pottery is also green to brown.

68

is difficult at best for the average plant. It must contend with unusual ranges of temperature and humidity, unnatural conditions of light, air, and sunshine. Consequently plants recommended for their ability to endure a household existence do not normally produce much bloom. The lack of flower hues restricts your choice of color in your container. Containers for planters should be inconspicuous in hue. They must share somewhat in the total effect but never be noticeable to the point of distraction. They are but a secondary part of the design. Their function is simply to hold the moisture and the earth for the growing plants. Containers of brown, gray, and muted greens, therefore, are best. Color exceptions, though not generally recommended, may sometimes be acceptable. A home with brass decorative features might include a brass planter; in a modified period home a pink alabaster urn could be exquisite if planted to all-white, or white-and-green variegated, foliage.

Containers may be round, square, or rectangular, but the depth is a very important dimension. The container must be never too deep, never too shallow. If it is too deep, the proper aeration of the earth cannot take place; if it is too shallow and too much air and water are present, root growth does not proceed properly. The best container is not under four inches nor over eight inches in depth, depending on the size of the bowl in relation to the surface expanse of earth. A container of very small mouth or surface expanse will not be successful, but a bowl with an eight-inch depth and a circumference for surface planting of twenty-four inches or more will afford ideal growth conditions.

The container may be of any suitable material. In making your selection you will be guided by the background of its location. Apart from this, you may choose freely in accordance with your personal taste.

SOIL PREPARATION

Different types of plants require rather specific soil mixtures. The usual procedure is to place one layer of coarse gravel in the bottom of the pot, then to fill with the type of soil suited to the plants to be set. A good all-around mixture that is safe for the average planter consists of two parts of peat moss, one part of leaf mold, and one part of sand. If the plant selection is entirely of cacti and succulents, the peat moss should be replaced with loam, and the leaf mold sharply reduced. For planters of ferns and other growth that need more humus, increase the leaf mold and add loam.

Do not set the plants deep in the container. Roots need room to grow, with plenty of soil below as well as around them. Do not fill the container to the rim.

SELECTION OF PLANT MATERIAL

When you select plant materials to combine in one container, your first important precaution is to use only those growths that require similar soil and moisture conditions. A planter consisting of cacti and succulents will have a sandy soil, and you will give very little moisture once growth is established. This planter must sit in full sun. On the other hand, you must place such moisture-loving plants as ivy, equisetum, maranta, and dracaena in a partially shaded area. They will need more frequent watering than the usual planter (Plates 39, 40). Plants using less moisture are those subject to rot or mildew, such as bamboo, sansevieria, and aralia (Plate 41).

THE DESIGN

As you arrange the plant material within the container, your knowledge of design will inspire you to compositional effects that are far more attractive than the standard plantings of the average commercial grower. If you plant carefully with the fashion of arranged cut material in mind, your designs will be lovely in form (Plate 42). Scale, however, is the most important principle to be observed. The size of the container places sharp limitations on the size of roots. This curb is really a protection, in that it prevents undue emphasis on height. Most of your plants are small, and many of the tiny ones are so exquisite that you will be tempted to an overlavish selection. The individual charm of these plants must not be accented to the detriment of the pattern. It is the over-all picture that counts. There are no other restraints on form in planter composition. Your awareness of subtle tonal values in green will guide you in color

PLATE 39

This is a very simple planter, but beautiful in the delicacy of the foliage. The tall vertical line is made with two varieties of small-leaved ivy. Although ivy is usually a trailing growth, in this design a slab of brown bark enables it to maintain its upright position. A miniature variety of dracaena is barely discernible behind the bark on the right of the ivy placement. Green-and-white variegated ivy is centered low for color interest and makes appropriate combination with the white-and-green flecked container.

PLATE 40

Equisetum, miniature ivy, and a small specimen of variegated dracaena compose this triangular grouping of plants. Centered directly in front of the bark slab is a clustering of white pebbles to suggest an outdoor location. In the far corners of the container tufts of moss conceal the earth.

PLATE 41

Miniature bamboo is one of the few tree growths you can combine with other plants in a movable container. You can clip its root system severely to prevent rapid growth; and it is sufficiently hardy to endure this drastic pruning. Only by the most heavy cutting can you maintain sufficient room in the soil content to nourish other plants.

PLATE 42

This planter is an excellent example of how you can apply principles of cut-flower design to the arrangement of growing plants. The symmetrical grouping employs a three-level pattern. Sprays of a succulent that permits moisture and branches of small-leaved ivy are the prominent placements in the composition. The intermediate areas are covered with a variety of small growing plants. The container is moss green. Whenever a planter is arranged for compositional effects, the lines of the pattern can be maintained by pruning and occasional manipulation.

74

combinations. In a pattern that stresses color, you will feature the rosettes and the leaves that are mottled yellow and green, or the variegated grasses with their clear green and white stripings. Many designers add accessories to these arrangements. Interesting forms and textures in rocks, bark, and driftwood increase the impression of landscape (Plate 40).

After the materials have been planted, after the earth has been firmly pressed down, watered, and settled, the surface of the exposed ground may be covered with moss or planted to miniature ground covers.

These planters are not lasting; they must be renewed at frequent intervals. A good planter, arranged knowledgeably, will live in good condition for six months to a year with no further concern than a little attention for watering.

PERMANENT PLANTERS

Permanent planters today are installed in any room. Sometimes in a house a portion of the earth is left exposed for planting, particularly if a tree can be permitted to grow out the roof top. The space immediately surrounding the trunk is given over to small plantings.

Planters that are a part of the construction of the house must be sizable to permit root expansion. Here, again, scale is the most important principle to observe. Wall areas, windows, or other features that serve as a background for the planter determine the vertical height or the horizontal spread of the materials to be planted. When a planter is used for a protective screen or a wall divider, the height of the plant is determined by the partitioning requirements of the room. The planter itself may be extremely long, yet narrow. A fast-growing tree, such as a rubber tree, can be used to achieve quick effects. The small, slow-growing plants that are desirable for movable planters are not suitable companions for the large growths of the permanent planter. In planters, just as in the outdoor garden, growth can be stimulated or retarded by the amount and the frequency of water and fertilizer supply.

CHAPTER V

Flowers and Foliage
of Quality or Distinction

VERY FLOWER has a horticultural personality. Even the most ordinary of flowers possesses an individual beauty suited to purposes of design. It does very well until brought beside a choicer blossom. The comparison may reveal some particular element of beauty which the first flower lacks but the second one possesses. It may be an exquisiteness of texture (Plate 43), a perfection of form and contour lines (Plate 44), or a delicacy of hue (Plate 45), or perhaps a summation of these qualities. At all events, one blossom is attractive, while the other is consummately beautiful.

It is not that the lovelier blooms are more difficult to grow; nor are they necessarily rare species. The wild flowers give us some of our loveliest blossoms; common garden-grown varieties sometimes produce flowers of such distinct shape, color, and texture that they seem too fair to touch.

It must be remembered also that what is called common in one community may be treasured floral material in another. Among the common varieties the individual blossom of the hollyhock is peerless. Its porcelain texture, the range of color and mottlings, give it an extravagant loveliness apparent in all its multifarious appearances. For it is a single flower, or it is double; it has plain or scalloped edges; it is lacy or firmly con-

PLATE 43

Foliage of heavy texture and interesting color has been chosen for the basis of this design. The leaves of epiphyllum have strongly indented outer edges. The heavy midrib is red-bronze. These qualities have been preserved in the drying process. A volcanic rock of triangular shape selected for its unusual texture hides the pin-type holder. Yellow-orange hibiscus blossoms and buds are set on the background of patterned leaves. Hibiscus blooms do not need water for their brief life span; but since they last for only one day, they must be replaced regularly.

PLATE 44

The material is arranged in silhouette pattern to provide a suitable background for the lilies. Epiphyllum blades, rose-pink to green, with gray ribbing, make the slender vertical placements. The exquisite rubrum lilies need no emphasis to reveal their beauty. With the most neutral material they create sufficient loveliness of their own. The container of shiny grayed-pink glaze was designed by the author.

PLATE 45

Blue agapanthus with its own green foliage is the subject matter
of this design. Umbels of clear blue make a dainty rounded pyramid
supported by the low, slanting placement of leaves. A delft blue container capped by a pin-type cup holder is the receptacle for the arrangement.

79

toured. In color it ranges from the lightest of tints to the deepest of shades, then to almost complete black. When stripped from its heavy stalk and ungainly foliage and used as an individual unit, it is entirely lovely. Yet in some regions where it grows in rank abundance, it is relegated to a back-yard corner to hide an unsightly fence.

The peony is another common flower of wide distribution. When its rough leaves have been removed, it displays a delicacy of texture not unlike the beauty of alabaster.

The dramatic red-orange and black Oriental poppy has petals of gossamer tissue, frail as spun silk, that give it the elegance of specimen material. Nearly all the bulbous flowers possess distinction. Their refinement, coupled with the wide range of their growth and seasonal flowering periods, make them indispensable for all flower arrangers. And there are many of them in the spring: the daffodils, both the common and the improved varieties (Plate 46); tulips, satin smooth and lustrous in the sunlight (Plate 47); hyacinths, overpowering in fragrance, carved from ivory; Dutch iris, whose petals of Wedgwood blue presage the later beauty of the bearded iris. All these greet the early spring among shrubs and trees as distinguished as their undergrowth. The magnolia soulangeana holds its rosy-purple cups to the sun; tasseled lilacs, the rhododendron, and the azalea float their evanescent perfume upon the garden air. Summer brings the hybrid hydrangeas, with their exquisite sterile beauty, and the magnolia grandiflora, noblest and grandest of garden trees. Lilies, again, resplendent with glowing color —day, tiger, gold-banded, and rubrum—splash their vivid hues against the border background. The greenhouse is bright with the sunset colors of the tuberous begonia. The waters of swamp or pond in late summer and fall shelter the most perishable jewels of all: the water lily, the Japanese iris, the blossoming lotus, and that exquisite pest, the gossamer, blue water hyacinth. In some outdoor gardens in America summer brings the agapanthus and the gorgeous hybrid amaryllis. Choice dahlias, such as the cactus type, qualify as flowers of distinction because of their rare colors and petal forms; also the highly developed strains of the chrysanthemum—the quill and the spider.

Because of the wide range of climatic conditions in the

temperate zone, some plants that are commonplace residents in the outdoor garden of the warm regions become subjects for the home greenhouse in the cooler areas. The list is long: the camellia, orchids, the blood lily, eucharis lilies, calla lilies (Plate 48), clivia, cyclamen, hibiscus, gingers, heliconia, the coral tree, and the hoya and the gloriosa vines. Some of the most spectacular plants should be grown only in the greenhouse: gloxinia, anthurium, spathiphyllum, and the stephanotis vine.

The appearance of choice blossoms in an arrangement of the home gardener is a triumph, for to grow them is a horticultural achievement of no mean proportions.

Flowers of Distinction

AGAPANTHUS	GOLD-BANDED LILY
AMARYLLIS	HELICONIA
ANTHURIUM	HOLLYHOCK
BANANA	HYACINTH
BILLBERGIA	IRIS
BIRD OF PARADISE	KNIPHOFIA
BLOOD LILY	LOTUS
BROMELIADS	NERINE
CACTUS	ORCHIDS
CALLA LILY	ORIENTAL POPPY
CEREUS	PEONY
CHRYSANTHEMUM	PETUNIA (DOUBLE)
CLIVIA	RANUNCULUS (HYBRID)
CYCLAMEN	ROSE
DAHLIA	RUBRUM LILY
DAY LILY	SPATHIPHYLLUM
DELPHINIUM (HYBRID)	TIGER LILY
EASTER LILY	TUBEROSE
EPIPHYLLUM	TUBEROUS BEGONIA
EUCHARIS LILY	TULIP
GINGER	VALLEY LILY
GLOXINIA	WATER LILY

Shrubs of Distinction

AZALEA	HYDRANGEA
CAMELLIA	LILAC
GARDENIA	POINSETTIA
HIBISCUS	RHODODENDRON

PLATE 46

 Daffodils and their own foliage form a double triangle. The void at the open end of the triangle is broken by two slender, pointed tips of leaves that carry the eye through the design without breaking.

This study shows how seemingly minor details can work homely material into distinguished compositions. Stalks of cane grass peeled to a layer of succulent brightness relieve the grayness of the artichoke placements. Looped grass leaves fatten the too-slender placements and balance the artichoke flowers. The splint basket container, set horizontally, also contributes.

PLATE 47

Six white tulips seem naturally placed in a delicate vase of hand-blown green glass. The blossoms are held in position by means of a wooden crotch set near the water line of the vase. The refinement and the simplicity of this pattern justify its use in a modern home of advanced design.

PLATE 48

The calla lily is a flower of distinction. From tightly furled bud to fully opened blossom, its form is beautiful. The velvet surface of the opened spathe is as lovely as its shape. The container of refined pottery is a soft mat glaze in textural harmony with the plant material.

84

Trees of Distinction

CORAL TREE	POINCIANA
DOGWOOD	SHOWER TREE
DOMBEYA	SOULANGEANA
EUCALYPTUS (SOME VARIETIES)	TULIP TREE

Vines of Distinction

BEAUMONTIA	MONSTERA
CLEMATIS	STEPHANOTIS
GLORIOSA	THUNBERGIA
HOYA	WISTARIA

Your foliage can be as distinguished as your flowers if you select your specimens carefully and regulate their growing conditions. Ivy, for example, is lovely in itself for its interesting form and deep green hue; but your designs become more exciting if you have the green and white variety, and still more unusual with the all-white kind (Plate 49). The ordinary green banana leaf, blown and tattered by the wind, is sufficiently exotic to provoke admiration. When, as in the Sumatra variety, it shows deep splotches of burgundy on its surface and satiny bronze on the under leaves, it is magnificent. You can find subtleties in the color and the form of foliage which approach the same qualities of distinction for which your treasured flowers are noted.

Foliage of Distinction

ACALYPHA	CASTOR BEAN (BROWN)
ACANTHUS	COLEUS
ALOCASIA	CROTON
ANTHURIUM CRYSTALLINUM	DIEFFENBACHIA
ANTHURIUM VEITCHII	DRACAENA
ANTHURIUM WAROCQUEANUM	EQUISETUM
ASPIDISTRA	GINGER (VARIEGATED)
BANANA	HELICONIA
BEGONIA (LARGE LEAF)	HOSTA
BROMELIAD	IRIS
CALADIUM (VARIEGATED)	IVY (VARIEGATED, WHITE)
CALLA LILY (YELLOW)	MAGNOLIA
CANE GRASS (VARIEGATED)	MARANTA
CANNA (BROWN)	NEW ZEALAND FLAX

PHILODENDRON	SPATHIPHYLLUM
RHOEO	UMBRELLA PLANT
SARRACENIA	VALLEY LILY

The unusual, the exotic, the unique, always attract. In the eighteenth and nineteenth centuries, the desire to own such plants, perhaps even to experiment with their growth, led to the construction of rooms called conservatories within the house. European homes of the very wealthy frequently held choice collections of exotic plants that could not endure the chill of European winters. The modern warm greenhouse is an unpretentious descendant of the conservatory. Many of these structures are small, but the control of temperature and humidity gives them a lively importance. You can derive as much pleasure here in the winter as your garden affords you during the warm months.

You must be careful to choose plants that require similar environment and group them with a thought for their habits and needs. Some must have light; they can be shelved high or hung in baskets. Shade-loving plants will sit under the benches.

Temperature is the most important factor. Since it will vary a few degrees in different sections of even the smallest greenhouse, you must regulate the temperature-control system for each part of the house if you are growing temperamental specimens. The cool greenhouse maintains a minimum night temperature of 45°–50°F; the warm-temperate greenhouse, 50°–55°F; and the tropical greenhouse, 60°–65°F. To simplify plant selection, you can establish a temperature zone of not less than 50°F, then restrict your choice to species that are happy in this environment.

In the cool greenhouse some kinds of orchid, the odontoglossum and suitable selections of cypripedium, are excellent companions, along with the bromeliads, favored because of their extremely handsome foliage. The caladiums, whose leaves are truly poetic in their coloring, will furnish a display satisfying to anyone. If you like greenery, some of the philodendrons make excellent cut foliage. The cool greenhouse, also, in climates too cold for outdoor growth, will house many of the distinctive plants that in warm areas can live outside. The bird of paradise (Plate 50), the beautiful lilies, and the clivia are

PLATE 49

One exquisite spray of ivory-green cymbidium orchids is held
in position by a Y-shaped holder set within a moss-green glass vase.
Two cuttings of green ivy are harmonious with the orchids in their
color, their shape, and their texture. This is material of true distinction
whose beauty is most clearly revealed through a design of complete
simplicity.

PLATE 50

The exotic bird of paradise, both foliage and blossoms, is presented in this design. The large leaves have been folded, then set in severely simple line placement. Vividly crested flowers wing out in dramatic repetition from the tall vertical. Even when such plant material has faded, its arresting pattern is still entertaining. The heavy pottery container on an attached base was designed by the author.

only a few. Begonias of all kinds, including the choice blooms of the tuberous-rooted, will be successful. Camellias and azaleas, if carefully selected, will provide blossoms from November through May.

Perhaps you prefer tropical plants. Anthurium is always a favorite with arrangers. Despite their size and the length of time required for propagation, orchids of the cattleya type are increasingly popular as home-grown rarities. Other orchids that need warmth are the lovely spray phalaenopsis, as well as the vanda. There are two kinds of cypripediums: one type prefers the cool greenhouse, the other needs warmth. Spathiphyllum, with its shiny green strap leaves and the white of the spadix, is a lovely thing. Heliconia and tropical ginger are most dramatic in the planter or in designs. Both the white and the yellow callas can be grown inside. For pronounced color the leaves of the croton give great variety; only the blue and the violet hues are missing. The starlike clusters of the ixora are so brilliant that it is commonly called "flame of the woods." Some of the new hibiscus are gorgeous; both the single and the double varieties have a purity of chroma that strengthens the delicate wrinkles of their papery texture. If you want poinsettias for holiday arrangements, both the single and the double types can be kept small as potted plants or allowed to grow to shrub size, depending, of course, on the size of the greenhouse. If there is space for vines, the bougainvillea—any one of the several colors—and the yellow or purple allamanda give a brilliant display.

With this extravagant range of potential beauty, only personal taste dictates the choice. What once was a narrow window shelf to hold one cherished plant has been enlarged until it is a controlled room providing a complete spread of yearlong beauty.

CHAPTER VI

Period Arrangements

THOUGH THE successful period arrangement is infrequently seen, it offers stimulating possibilities if you want to try something a bit different from your usual designs. It always makes a fitting complement to a period room or a piece of period furniture; yet it can be used without any discordance in the modern setting. The bouquet-makers of past centuries worked in happy ignorance of the rules and principles of design. They did not attempt an arrangement. They set flowers in a vase— because they possessed choice blossoms or unusual specimens selected probably for beauty of color. And the ordinary vaseful held a goodly assortment. You will not often attempt such lavish grouping. But if you fashion a period pattern, you should provide a spot of ripe color attractive enough to set before a paneled background or to brighten an area of neutral colors devoid of ornamentation. You will encounter fewer difficulties if you understand the historical background of your period. For you will wish your floral piece to be a reasonably authentic expression of the age you have selected, as well as artistically satisfactory for the twentieth century. The principles of modern design are not numerous, but they are demanding; and their development and formulation go a long way into the past.

THE RENAISSANCE

It is difficult to conjecture what the modern art world would have been without the great period of the Renaissance. Our immediate association with the word "Renaissance" is Italy. But it was a very complex Italy. Scholars from the Byzantine East, from Constantinople and Damascus and Baghdad, flocked into Italy with their precious hoard of treasures. Sudden discoveries of classical learning long forgotten, from ancient Greece and Rome, astonished and delighted the rulers of the powerful states of Italy. The Medicis of Florence, the dukes of Ferrara and Genoa—to cite but a few—vied with each other in offering patronage to artists who could beautify their cities. The rich and influential families spent lavishly of their wealth for the adornment of their palaces and churches. Painters, sculptors, and goldsmiths wrought such works of permanent beauty that Italy became the source of inspiration for the Continent; and from Italy the great revival of learning and of beauty spread throughout Europe.

Minor certainly among the subjects of Renaissance treatment but nevertheless of genuine interest was the use of flowers as adornment. Garlands and festoons of fruit and flowers were used in mural decorations; for picture frames; as details in paintings; as trimmings for pageants, festivals, and dramatic entertainments.

The Renaissance is noted also for the extravagant beauty of its fabrics. The textile-weavers, especially those of Italy and the Low Countries (the present Netherlands and Belgium), had long been famous for their workmanship and designs. Inspired by the discoveries in ancient classical learning, they set aside many of the familiar motifs popular during the Middle Ages and substituted the classic details of the acanthus, the iris, and the lotus. The French weavers turned to floral models close at hand in the royal gardens and wrought the flowers and the ferns of their own country into rich cloths (Plate 51).

Wherever it appeared throughout the continent of Europe, the Renaissance exhibited similar characteristics; yet there were local distinctions of great significance caused by circumstances peculiar to each country. Spain, for example, shows less of Italian influence than does any other area because of its long period of Eastern domination—for over eight hundred years Spain was ruled by the Saracens, then the Moors, and finally by the Ottomans or Turks. Spanish art, therefore, was largely Oriental in its mood. When the Spanish Renaissance began, it was initiated chiefly from the Low Countries, Netherlands and Flanders, with whom Spain had economic and political connections.

In England the Renaissance was even more modified than it was in Spain. According to the historians the English Renaissance begins with Henry VIII and extends through the Stuart period. The early years were given over to an intensive study of Italian models. Italian artists and workmen came to England and introduced Italian styles. Henry's quarrel with the Pope, his divorce, and the change of state religion sent the Italians home. They were replaced by Flemish artists and artisans, with a consequent shift in art motifs. Later, at the end of the period, French influence was uppermost.

It is, then, highly improper to regard the Renaissance as a clean-cut, unified movement that steadily progressed from Italy throughout the Continent. It did unquestionably lay the foundations for the succeeding periods of art; but because of its shifting character it was modified everywhere by local circumstance. These events, political and economic, were sometimes of long, sometimes of short, duration. Occasionally the economic or social forces coincided with the political and can be measured in decades or reigns. But much more often, through a gradual tapering, they imperceptibly blended into the forces that succeeded them, and there was frequently an age so confused that any arbitrary naming is certain to be criticized. The historical nomenclature is determined entirely by political divisions—Georgian, Directoire, Empire, Colonial, Federal, all these terms are unmistakably clear in the history books. When applied to art forms of any sort, however, they are misleading and should be used with the greatest discretion. Consider, for example, the work of Sir Christopher Wren and the master carver Grinling Gibbons. Sir Christopher, the architect extraordinary of St. Paul's Cathedral in London, lived toward the end of the English Renaissance. He had studied in Paris and was thoroughly imbued with the ideals of the French Renaissance. He had, indeed, become so French in his taste that his own style in decoration is profuse with ornamentation of fruit and flowers. Grinling Gibbons, who did much of this elaborate carving, was employed by Charles II to carve foliage and fruit in work on the royal palace. Later he was master carver to George I. This

PLATE 51

An arrangement of delicate dignity has been developed in pale pink amaryllis set very simply in a gray chalice. The lightness of the color scheme suggests the paintings of Botticelli. Italian Renaissance art inspired the entire composition; for the container was copied by the author from a Renaissance pattern.

type of work made famous by Wren and Gibbons is frequently labeled Georgian. It was developed, however, under Renaissance influence and in the latter part of the English Renaissance. We think of the Renaissance and the Georgian periods as being widely separated; yet in this incidence they are clearly related. How difficult it is, then, to make a cleavage between periods that stand close in time and space, and how misleading to attempt a sharp division.

DUTCH AND FLEMISH BAROQUE: SEVENTEENTH AND EIGHTEENTH CENTURIES

The flower arranger usually begins period study with the work of the Dutch and Flemish artists of the seventeenth and eighteenth centuries. They employed a restrained baroque style which, like so many art influences, had originated in Italy and spread throughout those parts of the Continent strongly affected by Italian trends. In definite contrast to the symmetry of the classic forms that the early Renaissance had striven to imitate, the baroque style is irregular. Because of its asymmetry, it is dynamic and energetic instead of stately and placid. It can most easily be illustrated by well-known architectural forms. During the late Renaissance Michelangelo departed from the restraints of the classical and employed rich curves. The new spirit can be seen in St. Peter's, where strong opposition of unbalanced masses and lines is apparent in the colonnades. In France the palace of Versailles and the colonnade of the Louvre present stately formal exteriors; but the richly decorative effects of the interiors culminate in scrollwork based on shell forms. In England the baroque can be seen in the historic Banqueting Hall at Whitehall and the ornamentation of St. Paul's Cathedral. In all these examples the baroque tendencies are regulated and disciplined. The wonderful ceilings of these buildings usually display border trims in flowing ornamentation rich with flower and fruit forms.

The more extreme form of baroque is seen in Spain. The Escorial, somewhat bewildering in its somber-walled hugeness, has at its entrance the concentrated adornment of churriguer-esque ornament. The luxuriance of the baroquelike forms developed in Spain by José Churriguerra can most easily be seen in Mexico, where they were widely adopted. Spanish fabrics of the late seventeenth century also display the overlavish use of scrolls and curves so that the flower forms are confused. The extravagance of unrestrained detail is what many people understand the word "baroque" to mean, for the term eventually came to designate that which borders on the grotesque and the corrupt.

As you investigate the Flemish and the Dutch artists of the seventeenth century, you find the beauty of baroque; some of them, you discover, made interesting use of flower forms within the paintings, as well as of flowers in still-life arrangements. Based on a bold use of curves, the lines of the arrangements produce a definite feeling of movement. Many of the flowers are large—anemones, hollyhocks, foxgloves, iris, marigolds, lilies —with branches of large-leaved foliage—peony and poppy leaves, castor bean, cannas—of strong form and color. The colors and the textures are as luxurious as the curving lines. Not pastels but middle values in warm hues suggest rich abundance with petal surfaces that are silken or velvet. These flowers are set in massive containers. Urns of metal and stone, fat, rounded flasks of porcelain and glass, even baskets, are seen in the flower pictures. The containers almost always are heavy and strong. Such arrangements were intended for placement in formal settings, sometimes on a table in a hallway, sometimes in a niche or against a wide panel, in the large handsome houses of the Flemish and Dutch landowners.

FRENCH ROCOCO: 1715–1774

The baroque art of the seventeenth century was followed by a style that developed and prevailed in France from the Regency until the era of the French Revolution. Like the baroque, it is based on curves. But where the baroque line makes a heavy, strong S-curve, the French curve is small, delicate, sometimes a shortened double curve like the edging of a sea shell or a water-worn rock. The abundance of short curving lines gives this French style its name, rococo, from *rocaille*, the French word for the ornamentation developed from the asymmetrical curves of the artificial rockwork and the pierced shell forms that delighted eighteenth-century tastes. There are extant innumerable specimens of eighteenth-century rococo floral art. Tapestries— the Gobelin among others—fabrics, and ceramics all show many bouquets. There are, also, flower prints as we have them today, usually of bouquets. The paintings of Watteau and Boucher portray the environment of the French aristocracy and the beauty of their gay life. During this period the rooms were delicate, rather than majestic. Decorative features were numerous and varied. Mirrors and elaborate chandeliers were used in great numbers. Small objects of porcelain and fragile china, often depicting shepherdesses and nymphs, formed charming accessories. The flowers were more dainty than those in the preceding period: carnations, small peonies, small poppies, morningglories, bachelor's-buttons, are found in the illustrations. Textures were fine and crisp. The colors also were refined: cool colors together with yellow were frequent; and the combinations were harmonious effects of closely related hues rather than dramatic contrasts. Containers were varied. The urns were more elegant and more delicate than those found in the Flemish pictures. Often they were made of crystal or porcelain, as well as of metal or marble. Epergnes of all shapes and sizes, most of them very complicated, were favorite table decorations. Bowls and vases of Chinese influence were used (Plate 53). While there had been some extremes of decoration during the late years of the reign of Louis XV, the close of the rococo era was distinguished by the refinement and the daintiness of Marie Antoinette. Her tastes were simple in contrast to the extravagance of the court of Louis XV, and it is this almost classic simplicity that forms the transition to the next period (Plate 54).

FRENCH NEOCLASSICISM: 1774–1814

In the late eighteenth and early nineteenth centuries the graceful rococo curves and asymmetric designs were gradually

PLATE 52

Flemish paintings of floral art are distinguished for lavishness of material and richness of coloring. This design was done after the manner of Bosschaert. It is composed necessarily of many flowers: canna blossoms, carnations, lilies, and roses, combined with crab apples. At the base of the large bronze urn are ripe peaches and shell forms that the Flemish delighted to show in their homes and their pictures.

PLATE 53

    This design has been copied from a detail in a Savonnerie tapestry. The curves of the rococo period are indicated in the graceful, trailing vines that bind the arrangement to the table. The plant materials are variegated ivy, carnations, roses, and lilies, all built into the curves of the pattern, either in the principal circular placements or as variation to the form. A large clustering of the star-of-Bethlehem is low in the composition and off-center. The urn is heavy marble. Shell relief extends the base of the urn in the rococo style.

PLATE 54

The floral material of this design was selected for its daintiness, to express the gaiety of the court of Louis XVI. The containers suggest the Cupid decorations at Versailles. These flowers were favorites in that era, but the pattern in which they have been arranged is not period style. It is purely imaginative. Pink miniature roses, lily of the valley, and white allium repeat the diagonal line of the Cupid's wings and bow. The vertical placement is made by the roses.

PLATE 55

　　This black and gold vase typifies both the Directoire and the
Empire periods. Since there are no recorded examples of flower arrangements during the Napoleonic era, this design is intended merely
to convey an idea of the masculine force prevalent at that time. The
palm, the fig, and the laurel were favored motifs. This pattern of fig
fruit and leaves is combined with heads of the star-of-Bethlehem whose
black centers echo the rich black of the container.

replaced by symmetry and straight lines. The discovery of Pompeii and its classic beauty fostered an enthusiasm for the ways of the past and restored an attention to symmetrical form. This neoclassical style prevailed during the Directoire and the Empire (Plate 55). Since the elegance of the period of Louis XVI and Marie Antoinette extended into the Directoire, this latter period possessed a distinction that is unusual in a period of such brevity. Noticeable immediately is the absence of any detail that would suggest royalty. Equally prominent is the replacement of the feminine refinement of Louis XVI furnishings with a more masculine quality. Napoleon favored two young architects, Percier and Fontaine, who developed the heavy Empire style—since their primary inspiration was Italy, particularly Rome. As Napoleon extended his conquests, decorative motifs from Egypt were added until a ceremonial style had been effected for public buildings which appears massive when compared with the greater elegance of the Directoire. Because the court atmosphere was definitely masculine, there is little pictorial record of flowers. Woven in the fabrics of the Empire were symbols of Napoleon's power—the lion, the sphinx, the eagle, wreaths indicating victory, and the golden bee, which was his personal emblem. The favorite colors were green or rose or royal purple, which made striking backgrounds for gold. Other colors were deep blues and reds. The rose seems to have been a favorite flower, together with plants reminiscent of classic taste, such as laurel leaves, wheat, anemones, and lilies. Classic fruits— pomegranates, quince, grapes, figs—arranged in bowls of Roman or Greek shape, in alabaster urns, porcelain bowls, and cornucopias, all heavy, express the spirit of the Empire.

GEORGIAN: 1714–1810

France in the Directoire had exhibited strong neoclassic tastes. This trend had appeared earlier in England. The Georgian period was characterized by its diversified taste in foreign influences. French, Italian, and Chinese styles, elaborately developed with rich accessories, were found in Georgian houses.

Early Georgian mural decoration in the style of Grinling Gibbons showed rich ornamentation of fruit and flowers patterned after French designs. Garlands of fruit and flowers carved above doors and fireplaces and on staircase supports were handsome whether wrought in wood or in plaster. This extensive use of flowers for mural display was in keeping with the eighteenth-century Englishman's love of gardening. Many of the great homes had elaborately designed grounds, usually in the formal manner learned in Italy. To record their beautiful flowers, the Georgians employed artists skilled in floral painting. Among those who came from the continent to make paintings and engravings were the Flemish artist Peter Casteels and the Dutch artist Jacob van Huysum. These prints with their deep, rich tones depict tulips, iris, marigolds and geraniums, pansies and violas, relieved by a few pale roses or daisies or stock. The containers are heavy urns of metal or marble, baskets, cups, and goblets (Plate 13).

The style of the late Georgian era was almost unrelieved neoclassic. Robert Adam designed magnificent houses that he decorated and furnished in stately elegance. Furniture by Hepplewhite, Chippendale, and Sheraton added further distinction. In the ceiling details Adam often used floral garlands, and he adorned the vast wall spaces either with painted panels displaying garlands and baskets of small flowers or, sometimes, with tapestries. The French Gobelin hangings with large arrangements of splendid floral design set in urns of classic pattern delighted the Georgians. The containers though simple in line were rather elegant in general appearance. Beautiful silver fruit dishes in Sheffield plate, shaped like Roman boats, or bowls with flaring edges, or baskets, were lovely for flowers. Josiah Wedgwood perfected processes by which he could produce antique effects that rivaled the finish of the real Greek and Roman pieces. He created a simulated porphyry; he brought out a line of luster finishes in green, gold, black, and agate. He designed containers and holders to fit his principles of arrangement which he had stated in a pamphlet, "The Art of Disposing the Most Beautiful Products of Nature." The containers were decorated with the classic motifs characteristic of Wedgwood ware.

VICTORIAN: 1830–1900

With the close of the Georgian period the creative fervor came to an end. The Romantic period of the nineteenth century produced splendid works of high originality in literature, but not in houses, furniture, or interior design. The Victorian era was a period of great economic success for the average man—resulting in an age of fat living. The abundance of all material objects led to overindulgence in the things that money could buy. House furnishings were too heavy and too cumbersome, curtains and draperies thick and unwieldy, furniture and bric-a-brac much too ornate with fat, puffy curves. Women wore too many clothes; they served overlavish, many-course dinners. Life was sheltered and handsome and righteous, but heavy; it did not promote a venturesome spirit.

As might be expected, the colors of the Victorian interiors were often as confused as the furniture. The rooms were large, but, since there was too much furniture, there seemed to be a lack of space. Table covers, usually of heavy velvet, carpets, curtains, draperies, wallpaper, upholstery, were in large, involved patterns. All were of bold, rich colors—deep blue, dark red and green, mulberry, purple, brown, gray, magenta—relieved by white, mustard-yellow, and pink. It was, then, hardly possible to decorate a room in a color scheme. The best one could do was to avoid clashes and select colors that would harmonize in their ponderous manner. Designers of real originality and unquestioned taste, such as William Morris, achieved extraordinarily pleasant effects despite the clutter.

The flowers of the Victorians were rich and heavy. Old-fashioned flowers with striped and spotted petals were favorites. Pansies and primroses, calceolarias and geraniums, foxgloves and cinerarias, variegated and striped carnations, camellias, and tulips—all these might be noticeable in arrangements, especially so when several kinds were combined in one bouquet. Full-bodied mass arrangements were usually triangular or circular, with flowers set closely to increase the mass effect until it often seemed top-heavy (Plate 56).

Containers of all shapes were used, many of them in bold colors embellished with heavy trimmings of gilt. Glass containers in very lovely colors and often of graceful shape were considered choice. Cast-iron urns, painted in white or brilliant colors, were as massive as the arrangements they held. Epergnes with flaring, trumpet-shaped tops were used when an unusually tall effect was desired. Along with these overrich designs was the tuzzy-muzzy, a small, neat arrangement with flowers in repeated circular lines, edged with foliage or lace or paper lacework. Sometimes one rose in the center was surrounded by other flowers. Often these tiny bouquets were set in little bouquet-holders of precious metal or enamel or porcelain and worn as ornament by a richly gowned Victorian lady.

EARLY COLONIAL: 1620–1700

Meantime in America a development very similar to the European stages had been taking place.

The word "colonial" has been carelessly applied to architecture and furnishings on the American continent prior to the organization of the American government. It could not, of course, have the same meaning in the several areas of early settlement. New England was established, for the most part, by the English of sober middle-class, often Puritanical tastes. The settlers of the Middle Atlantic sections were largely Quaker or Dutch. The South had a high percentage of Royalists and Cavaliers from England, who were strong exponents of the French style to which they had been accustomed at home. From the beginning, consequently, we find a very cosmopolitan spread of styles.

For the first few decades the houses were built in the simplest designs. The necessities of environment compelled a straight-line structure with spare ornamentation, so that both the house and the furniture were severe. New England had many skilled craftsmen who made expert use of native wood. Their models were what they knew of European design. We have few records of floral decoration. When the colonists had time to make bouquets, they possessed delightful possibilities for containers in the mugs and cups, pitchers and jugs, of everyday use. These were peasant-ware effects of English pottery and Dutch delft-ware (Plate 57).

PLATE 56

This arrangement is a direct copy of a Victorian design taken from one of the floral prints. The container of fine porcelain is hand-painted and depicts romantic figures in medallion effect surrounded by a floral garland. The flowers and their rich hues were beloved by the Victorians, who liked nothing better than great, full masses of color. Foliage sprays of abelia, dark red roses, fuchsias, petunias, purple-and-yellow pansies, and the red-orange blossoms of the epidendrum orchid make a robust pattern as full as the voluminous skirts and drapes of the period.

PLATE 57

A *brass-banded wooden mug could have been found, perhaps, in many homes of the American colonists. Bright red geraniums, we know, were highly prized decorations in those early kitchens. This casual arrangement suggests the untrained informality prevalent among the first Americans.*

Plants were cultivated principally for use, but most settlers made some attempt at flower gardens, with a few English plants scattered among the native ones they found. Within a very short time so many flower discoveries had been made that garden plots flourished.

LATE COLONIAL: 1700–1780

The true colonial style, an outgrowth of American ways of living and a development of American tastes, was not apparent until the beginning of the eighteenth century, and is contemporaneous with the Georgian period in England. By this time many of the colonists were exceedingly well-to-do, with homes of good lines and appointments. The rooms were not so large as those in English Georgian houses, but they were well finished. Beautiful native woods and an increasing supply of imported goods contributed to the handsomeness of the interiors. Wall panels were in natural finish, waxed and rubbed to a soft sheen; or they were painted, sometimes in white or delicate tints of ivory or buff, sometimes in tones of blue or green. Toward the end of the century lighter tints prevailed. Wallpapers and textiles were similar to those used in England. Furniture was elegant. Chippendale was the favorite style; and chairs, tables, sofas, and chests of mahogany were both imported and created by American craftsmen. Again, we have almost no records of colonial flower arrangements, but we know that beautiful containers were available: the pottery of the earlier period; porcelain and bone china from the Continent; some metal, especially silver. Paul Revere's fine workmanship must not be overlooked.

FEDERAL AND EARLY REPUBLIC: 1789–1830

The Federal period may be considered to extend through the first quarter of the nineteenth century. The neoclassic influence still persisted. The neat symmetry of classic design appeared in the formal elegance of many interiors that were decorated with trimmings and accessories of a mixed sort. The American eagle was used, as was a circle of golden stars or balls that indicated the thirteen states of the new republic. New, also, were increasingly large numbers of bowls and ceramic pieces brought in sailing vessels from China. French influence on American style was to be expected because of the part that France had played in the Revolutionary War. American fashions ran briefly through the changing styles of the exquisite delicacy of Marie Antoinette, the classic taste of the Directoire, and the heaviness of the Empire.

All this can be seen in the designs of Duncan Phyfe. His early furniture, modeled after Hepplewhite and Sheraton, though with considerable modification, was followed by much more substantial pieces. The neoclassic influence, both Georgian and French, shows also in the wide variety of containers: English china, Sheffield and Paul Revere silver, and lusterware. For the first time glass in considerable quantity was available, since beautiful and characteristic American glass was now manufactured.

These classic ideas of the new republic were followed, as in England, by the stuffiness that we associate with the Victorian age.

CHAPTER VII

Placement
and Special Occasion
Arrangements

FLOWERS DECORATE a room beautifully, but they should not be permitted to overbalance the furnishings. When a house is dressed up too much, it loses its air of casual or informal living. The mellowness of home is most easily secured through the use of branches and foliage, which remain attractive for long periods with little care (Plate 38).

In determining the placements for the designs, you should analyze each room. Study the color of the walls, the style of furniture, the color of the wood and the upholstery, and any hangings, pictures, lamps, or other accessories to determine whether or not the inclusion of outdoor beauty will benefit the room.

ENTRYWAY

When space permits, the entryway should always have an arrangement. When the front hall is properly dressed, it expresses far more than a correct grouping of plant material. It voices a greeting of friendliness; it expresses your way of life.

Most twentieth-century homes have an informal entrance. An unbalanced grouping of furniture—a chest off-center, a table and one chair, or unevenly spaced wall areas—looks best when completed with an arrangement of asymmetrical pattern (Plate 58). If limited space permits only a hanging shelf or wall bracket, make a design of the same type but in small scale (Plate 59).

Whenever the entrance to the house is formal, the furniture will be symmetrically placed. Perhaps a table is centered against a wall, flanked by a chair on either side; or a pedestal is centered; or two pedestals are set one either side of a panel. Your design in plant material should have the same equality of balance (Plate 11). Should you use two arrangements, they must be identical. If you prefer a variation of this highly symmetrical floral design, you can place two asymmetrical designs in opposition. They will be alike, though in reverse position, one a right-hand, the other a left-hand, design. When placed together, the two combine as one form in symmetry (Plate 60).

LIVING-ROOM

THE MANTEL

A fireplace in the living-room centered on its wall space requires symmetrical floral design on the mantel beam (Plate 9). If a mirror, a painting, or other accessory occupies this central space, two arrangements identical in pattern but reversed in position will be placed toward the ends of the mantel, one on either side of a central object (Plate 35). When the fireplace is off-center, the plant material will be grouped more informally; it will be set, perhaps, to one side of the mantel beam and balanced by accessories (Plate 23).

Because the fireplace is the heart of the room, you cannot embellish a mantel appropriately with flowers; you need a more forceful display. Magnolia or pine branches trimmed for pattern effect will do splendidly. Switches of pussy willow or genista, and cut foliage such as aspidistra, dracaena, or ivy, conform to the tailored lines of plain wood.

PLATE 58

An asymmetrical pattern of red-flowered Japanese quince establishes the form of this design. Three white hyacinths surrounded by
their own foliage and realistically grouped as in true growth are an important accent to this springtime composition. The arrangement has
been planned for a narrow table in an entrance hall.

PLATE 59

A vertical design requiring little space is good for the entryway to a small house or apartment, or for shelf decoration. Flowers and leaves of the common narcissus have been manipulated into this pattern. The column has been made to lean slightly to the left to provide balance for the deep curl of the leaves at the right. The lower curve, immediately above the tip of the flowers, stabilizes the design. The container is black glass.

PLATE 60

A home of extreme formality requires classic decoration. Two
black and gold urns hold matching designs of choice flowers: branches
of lilac, scilla, and lily of the valley with its foliage, completed with an
accent placement of blue-violet iris, both blossoms and bud. If moved
closer together, the two asymmetrical arrangements would combine as
one formal triangle. Set apart as they are, they suggest formal balance.

113

PLATE 61

Two flat arrangements can be used on a low coffee table. Durable material is preferable, particularly if worked into a design that will permit of modification from time to time. Leaves of the magnolia have been inserted into two pin-type holders, overlapped at their base, and furled back into loop position at their facing edges. This framework will last. The beautiful surface of the leaves makes an attractive frame for whatever blossom is featured.

114

THE OCCASIONAL TABLE

A small table in the living-room sometimes takes an arrangement scaled in size to the surface of the table. Be cautious in setting flowers on tables. Tables have been placed in the room to serve definite needs, perhaps to hold ash trays or magazines. A low, large table is a suitable location for one good design. The arrangement may be moderately high. More practical, however, is a low arrangement planned for the pleasure of those who are seated. If it is built in silhouette, the flower or leaf placements will be visible from both ends and on either side (Plate 5). Two matching low arrangements are practical if they do not seem to dwarf the table. You can establish a pleasing harmony of texture if you select foliage whose surface accords with the finish of the wood. A glossy-textured leaf pattern on a table of high polish is a decorative detail of elegant distinction (Plate 61).

In a large room a corner fireplace at one end can be balanced by an arrangement in the corner diagonally opposite. An occasional table can function nicely in a corner placement of this sort (Plates 62, 63).

THE PIANO

An upright piano is not a sensible place for decoration, but a grand piano in a large room will give attractive support to an arrangement. There is space for effective design, even for dramatic treatment. When a room contains both mantel and grand piano, and the piano is far removed from the fireplace, the arrangement on the piano should echo the mantel decoration. The curves of the piano case can be repeated in a circular floral pattern.

DINING-ROOM

Furniture groupings in the dining-room are standardized. Normally they consist of the dining-table and chairs in the center, the buffet at one side or one end of the room, balanced by the serving-table opposite. When this room is not being used as a dining-area, the buffet is a suitable location for an arrangement, perhaps a design of fruit asymmetrically patterned (Plate 64).

DINING-NOOK

A small room adjacent to the kitchen, or a part of the kitchen, makes an intimate dining-area for the family. Breakfast, irregular meals, and after-hour snacks are enjoyed there. Because of its informality a casual floral design will add charm and intimacy (Plate 65).

If the materials used in these arrangements for the home are to come from your garden, you must plant foliage that harmonizes with the wood of your furniture. The reddish-brown Japanese plum and canna of the same hue are beautiful with mahogany or cherry (Plate 66). Walnut, oak, birch, or maple call for the green-leaved variety of plants and trees (Plates 20, 37).

CHURCH

Flower arrangements for the church vary according to the architectural plan of the building. Since most churches are formal, the flower arrangement will be symmetrical. It will be placed above or below the pulpit or communion table (Plate 67).

When two arrangements are required, they may be asymmetrical like the mantel designs. This is the style to be used when two arrangements are placed one on either side of a central cross (Plate 68). You must make sure that the vertical and the horizontal placements of the designs will not slip from position. Use some mechanical device to hold the stalks in place if the containers are slender-throated vases. Fine wire mesh cut in small pieces, then crushed and thrust into the containers, will serve in any opaque material, such as the vases of gold or brass traditional for church decoration. Also, for narrow-

PLATE 62

A small occasional table set in a corner is a good location for this tall arrangement. A cylindrical vase of brown pottery holds delicate apricot branches whose brown stems continue the hue of the container. The mauve shadings of the soulangeana magnolia match the color variations in the textured background of the curtains. The effect is delightfully springlike.

PLATE 63

　　Folded leaves of the green canna successively shortened to suggest a spiraling effect provide a framework that reaches from the tip of the tallest leaf to the very short placement at the right. Three loops of green-and-white striped cane grass on the right balance the canna leaves. Within this spiral are blossoms of the quill chrysanthemum, their clear white a lovely accent against the brilliant green of the foliage. This arrangement is beautiful from any point of view. The container is a pottery piece of soft green mat glaze designed by the author.

PLATE 64

An extremely tall brass compote holds a grouping of exotic
fruit. An avocado branch of fruit and leaves trails over the edge, a pineapple is centered, and bananas provide transitions within the design.
The arrangement is planned for a buffet table at one end of the dining-
room. It is so spectacular in line and color that it affords pronounced
decorative effect.

PLATE 65

This container is an authentic Dutch wooden shoe. Shapely cups of tulips are set in a gentle curve that is finished by the opened blossom at the base; and looped leaves complete the composition with a gay flourish. Such a design may be placed on a window ledge or a table in the kitchen.

PLATE 66

   Leaves of the red canna have been furled, folded, and curved to
provide an interesting depth of planes for this composition. Sprays of
Japanese plum make the horizontal base. The pattern is extremely
dignified, as is usual with the L-shaped design; and the color relationship is deep and rich: red-burnished canna, mahogany plum leaves,
mahogany-colored wooden base.

PLATE 67

A *church arrangement may be elaborate. Usually it is built with more material than is put in a decoration for the home. If the church is small and only one design is used, it must be large enough to seem to decorate the entire room. Above all else it must be dignified. An alabaster vase makes a beautiful and highly suitable container. Three stalks of acanthus in flower, sprays of viburnum beginning to blossom, white trumpets of beaumontia, and loquat leaves form this symmetrical pattern.*

PLATE 68

Two right-angled patterns are set at either side of the cross for altar placement. The vertical and horizontal lines are sharply delineated in order that their forms may be visible from every point of view. The two arrangements repeat the symmetry of traditional background features.

PLATE 69

This plate illustrates more clearly the triangular feature suggested in Plate 68. These are the same arrangements shown in the preceding plate. Branches of pomegranate make the vertical and horizontal lines. Cuttings of variegated pittosporum are clustered at the tip of the vases. Short branches of the same pittosporum held in a very narrow vase behind the cross complete the triangle design.

124

necked containers, select flowers with firm, slender straight stems for these major placements of vertical and horizontal lines. Thin stems of aspidistra, privet, and ligustrum are suitable foliage materials.

The presence of the cross does not affect the height of the arrangement. Should you feel that your design would be more beautiful if extended above the cross, there is no reason why you should not follow your inclination. Flowers and other plant material have always been used very freely around or above the cross (Plate 69).

The material used in church decoration should not be stereotyped. All material in natural supply is suitable. Sprays of berried shrubs, vegetables and fruits arranged casually or stylized after the manner of the della Robbias, gilded and metallic leaves and branches, such as the palm frond, and even a motif of stars and tinsel to embellish the glory of the Christmas arrangements—all are appropriate combinations for church decorations.

If the structure of the church is not symmetrical, you have more freedom in using varied forms and lines in the single arrangement. It may be circular, horizontal, triangular, or vertical. Its proportions need not be limited to the background of the altar space. Although it should be arranged to a scale suitable to the size of the room, you are free to emphasize any proportion of the design (Plate 3).

WEDDING DECORATIONS

THE CHURCH

White is the traditional color for church decoration, although weddings of great splendor frequently deviate from the accepted pattern.

The number of floral arrangements will depend upon the simplicity or the elegance of the wedding. The altar decorations or frontal placements usually remain the same as for normal church services. However, the area near the altar railing or the termination of the central aisle where the ceremony takes place provides opportunity for additional arrangements on columns or pedestals. Standing candelabra elaborate this setting. All-white arrangements should be backed with long fronds of fern or long sprays of other evergreen material whose tips project to outline the white material of the design. This is the standard setting for church weddings. Should more splendor be desirable, the ends of the pews on the central aisle can be finished with tied sprays of white flowers backed with foliage. The side windows can also be banked at the base with window box effects. More elaborate decorations follow this same plan for floral placement. A color other than white can be used in a motif expressive of the season or in harmony with a color dominating the church.

For an all-pink spring wedding the placements are made of pale pink flowering peach. Even the rafters are loosely interlocked with large branches, so that falling petals softly filter down upon the guests. The bridal party carries hyacinths and tulips arranged so casually that they might have been picked by the attendants themselves. The whole effect expresses the theme of pastoral beauty in springtime.

For a fall wedding the traditional front placements are rich arrangements of fruit and foliage. The stained-glass windows are outlined with tailored garlands of fruit and magnolia leaves in the yellow-to-persimmon hues of autumn. Long, narrow garlands are fashioned in the technique of the fruit and leaf combination illustrated in Plate 70. The velvet-frocked bridal party carry chrysanthemums festooned with long bunches of grapes.

Decorations in the church for a wedding during the yule season consist of fir trees embellished with poinsettias. The white-frocked attendants carry lighted candles held in position by sprays of heavily berried holly and vivid-red streamers.

THE HOME

When planning decorations for the home wedding, select a balanced wall area. If this wall has a centrally located fireplace, the setting is ideal. One large design in formal balance can be centered, or the mantel can be trimmed with a horizontal banking. Two occasional tables or pedestals supporting matched arrangements should flank the fireplace. Standing candelabra can be used with this grouping. Fill in or cover the open burning-area with cut fern or other greens.

When a balanced fireplace and mantel are not available, a

PLATE 70

To devise a door treatment of this garland type, wire each magnolia leaf with a medium-weight florist's wire fourteen or sixteen inches
long. Insert toward the stem end of the leaf. Bend the wire at mid-
length; then each leaf will have a double wire seven inches in length.
Place the leaves in position, overlapping in shingle fashion, fastening
each wire to the one adjoining, increasing the width of the design as
leaves are added. The wiring and the assembling are done as in making
a corsage. The small orange-colored Italian limes are wired individually
in the same manner, clustered in groups, and added near the top of
the design. A bow of orange ribbon with streamers cut diagonally
completes the arrangement.

section of the wall with evenly spaced windows or doors provides a balanced setting. One symmetrical arrangement on a tall centered column simulates the mantel beam (Plate 11). This can be strengthened by the two lower placements and the candelabra that were suggested for paralleling the fireplace. Greenery arranged at the base completes the decoration.

THE TABLES

The table-setting is planned with consideration for the hour. Breakfast or luncheon tables are less flowery than those arranged for the afternoon or evening reception. In every case the elaboration of the decorations is determined by the size of the affair and the number of guests.

Even for a small wedding party with the guests seated, it is not customary to place the wedding cake on the main table. Use, instead, a simple floral design. Probably the cake has been placed on another table.

For the large wedding reception three tables are used. One table is centered with a flowery display flanked by the coffee and the tea services at either end. The champagne table holds the silver punch bowl, with an elaborate design on either side. The cake occupies a third table whose shape corresponds to that of the cake. For the circular cake a false round top is placed over a square table. The cloth may be of sheer material, very fluffy, or tailored in heavy satin. If the table is square, the cloth caught with clusters of flowers at the four corners of the table is decorative. Outline the base of the cake with loose heads of delicate blossoms, with perhaps a clustering of similar flowers on top.

Regardless of the hour of a wedding party, lighted candles may be used on any of the decorated tables.

THE GARDEN PARTY

A garden is a beautiful location for a wedding reception or the wedding itself, as well as for the conventional garden party.

The garden must be prepared. Prune all overhead branches

and hanging vines to ensure sufficient headroom for guests. The walks should likewise be freed of any encroaching lateral branches that may snag a frock. Go through the garden appraising each area and studying each specimen. Prune shrubs and trees to give them interesting line, or precise stylization if the garden is the formal kind. If the occasion is a wedding, save all the branches that have been cut in the pruning to use as backing for a frontal screen.

The loveliest setting for the garden wedding is an area approached by a formal walk. Then the guests will enter by way of an aisle bordered by a planting that has been symmetrically spaced and pruned. Clipped boxwoods two by two, or tree roses, or any other matched planting makes an avenue of proper dignity. When the background planting is informal and natural, it is a simple matter to rent or to buy stylized plants in tubs. Set them on the ground or bed them down in the sod to provide this formal walk.

You are now ready to work the garden beds. They should be immaculate. Where the soil has hardened, even though it may be free of weeds, it should be reworked so that every bed is softened with fine loam to make a suitable background for the flower shrub areas.

After this preliminary work has been accomplished, set the outdoor furniture and other garden accessories where they will be available when needed and yet will give a lived-in aspect. When the guest list is not too large, arrange the furniture in casual groups near the improvised altar, not too close and yet within hearing distance of the ceremony. This furniture grouping gives a much better appearance than folding chairs in rows. An informally natural effect is important for the afternoon wedding.

For the evening wedding with a large guest list the seating-area should be formally arranged as in a church with only a central aisle for the entrance of the bridal party. For the reception, move some of the chairs to the place where refreshments are served and cluster them informally for those who prefer to be seated.

You may wish to increase the display in the garden borders or the bedding-area with a profusion of bloom. An elaborate floral effect can be secured very easily by placing potted plants concealed by the natural, growing ground cover or by burying the pots where they are needed.

Important areas may require final embellishment on the day of the wedding. The formal walk of tree roses can be given a profuse display of color. To supply additions that will last briefly, wire on cut flowers. Because they will be without water after they have been wired to the bush, they must be carefully conditioned. Be sure that the stems have been immersed for several hours up to the heads of the flowers, or even immerse the flowers completely so that they will be very crisp. To attempt to wire water-filled test tubes on the shrubs requires a great deal of time. It is also very difficult to conceal these tubes. If they are even slightly visible, their disclosure will completely ruin the illusion of a shrub in its glory of full bloom. If the formal path is bordered with camellia bushes instead of roses and the season is past, use any disk flower that looks well with camellia foliage. Flowers similar to those used for the aisleway shrubs will be wired to the branches at the frontal bower to give unity to the garden setting. This artificial wiring should be done when the sun is low; then spray the attached blooms occasionally with a very fine mist until just before the wedding.

If the garden is used only for the reception but not for the wedding ceremony, wired-on blossoms are rarely employed. The reception calls for spectacularly beautiful flower arrangements or interesting groups of potted plants rather than elaborate plantings.

A charming and colorful entryway decoration can be made with a wheelbarrow holding large flowers. The arrangement must be in scale to the size of the improvised container (Plate 71).

Spacious gardens often include a lake or a large pond with a small boat for fishing. This setting for an arrangement is original and beautiful. Sumptuously decorated, the boat can be very lovely as it floats above its reflection in the water (Plate 72).

The swimming pool should be dressed for the occasion. Group water lilies naturalistically, then make them secure with weights to hold their position in the pool. Gardenias and other blossoms managed in a similar manner give charming water effects. Clear rubber or plastic balloons, also weighted, and

This arrangement is an interesting study in proportion. The dominant branch of stock was selected for the unusual blending of its stem, a curve that suggested an appropriate pattern. Close clustering of the florets gives sufficient substance to stand as the only vertical placement and support for the figurine. A spaced disposition of the open cyclamen flowers widens the base to a stable foundation for the heavy stock. The two slender buds direct attention to the Madonna.

PLATE 71

For the garden party toward the end of summer a wheelbarrow loaded with choice specimens from the vegetable garden makes a novel design. Cornstalks are used for the wide, airy placements, with whatever vegetables are at hand. A few blossoms of giant dahlias add color interest and provide transition from the cornstalks to the small vegetables. Garden tools add a practical touch to this arrangement that will be set at the side of a garden path.

131

PLATE 72

Another charming arrangement for a large garden with a pond or small lake can be placed in a boat. Here a massive design of tall brown canna leaves, orange canna blossoms, and large dahlias fills the space between decks. The coolness of the water with its pads of water lilies and green reflections make a delightful conversation spot for garden-party guests.

132

scattered among the flowers, look like the luminous floats of fish nets. For the lighted pool and night effects, you must wax the water-lily blooms to keep them open after dark. The procedure is first to wax heavily the center stamens, and then to drop wax at the base of each petal, finishing each whorl of petals and gradually descending to the final whorl of green sepals.

Satirical arrangements lend whimsical charm. A design of choice garden vegetables about to be attacked by an enormous green raffia grasshopper is suited to a casual grouping of table and chairs (Plate 73). Just as effective in its mirth-making intent is a little papier-mâché snake on the liquor bar. It should be partially concealed, as in nature, by equisetum and the stump and bark of a dead tree (Plate 74). Endless opportunities present themselves for novel decorations (Plate 75).

Garden affairs should be planned only for the season of outdoor comfort. If you entertain frequently in your garden, you will plant shrubs, trees, and perennials that will reach their perfection when your garden is open for hospitality. In very early spring in some sections of the United States the pathways are outlined by camellias in abundant pink bloom. The underplanting is of pink azaleas so that the entire walk is a harmony of one color to delight visitors. Another garden will be open when the tall blue jacaranda trees are in full bloom and the lower borders reflect the same hue from the agapanthus. Hydrangeas in a blending of orchid and blue color the intermediate height from tree to agapanthus.

BIRTHDAYS

A floral offering makes an appropriate gift for a friend whose desires and tastes are not well known. Loose cut flowers can be very beautifully boxed. Place each layer of flowers on little lace paper mats and tie the box with elaborate ribbon effects. These are festive touches that the professional florist cannot always take the time to give unless a gift wrap has been specifically ordered. Or set the flowers within a container, displaying the best of your creative ability. You should send only very choice flowers as a gift (Plate 76).

CHRISTENINGS

A christening can be an elaborate affair. Flowers or flower arrangements sent to the home are more pretentious than the small-scale, sweet little offerings sent at birth. They should be sufficiently decorative to function on the feast table or as complement to the home during this fete (Plate 11).

GRADUATIONS

Although most schools have discontinued the tradition of sending flowers to the graduate, in some communities and in some private schools the custom still prevails. When flowers are sent or taken, they should be timed to arrive in advance of the graduation exercises. The arrangement should be elegant: a colorful bouquet of the choicest flowers tied with ribbon or tulle.

HOUSEWARMINGS

Housewarmings provide an excellent opportunity for the giving of flowers, especially when the specific wants of the new owners are unknown to the guest. If it is possible to learn the color schemes of the various rooms, an arrangement planned to harmonize is a thoughtful expression (Plate 62).

ILLNESS

The selection of flowers for a person confined to a sickroom calls for the exercise of good judgment. Heavy fragrances and vivid colors should be avoided. Restful, yet cheering colors should be blended into an interesting composition. The inclusion of several different kinds of flowers with subtle variations in size and texture often gives the most satisfaction to the in-

PLATE 73

Garden-party guests enjoy the humorous as well as the beautiful. A metal table near the stream holds a mirth-provoking design. The container is a hollowed tree branch, weathered and gray, filled with freshly cut vegetables. Tall stalks of celery, a few onions whose tops have been clipped, and a full, round head of lettuce attract a grasshopper. His grotesquely exaggerated body and his long legs and wing cases are made of green raffia so bright that he is easily conspicuous from a distance.

PLATE 74

Furled bark has been manipulated to resemble a rotted tree stump with cavernous openings. Set upright to serve as a vertical placement, it is supported by slender rods of equisetum which appear to be growing behind a triangular bit of driftwood. A low bowl with pin-type holders for the equisetum is conveniently located behind the driftwood. A little green water snake is inquisitively eying the water that must be present wherever equisetum grows.

PLATE 75

*A whimsical arrangement certain to provoke comment at a
garden party has been set in a low, flat basket of yellow raffia. Sprays
of Scotch broom with a scattering of its bright yellow blossoms make
the tall, airy placements. Daffodils and their leaves complete the floral
design. The foot of the stems is concealed by a knot of brown wood.
In front are two bees of yellow and brown raffia, whose imposing size
and conspicuous coloring will attract the attention that the designer
intended.*

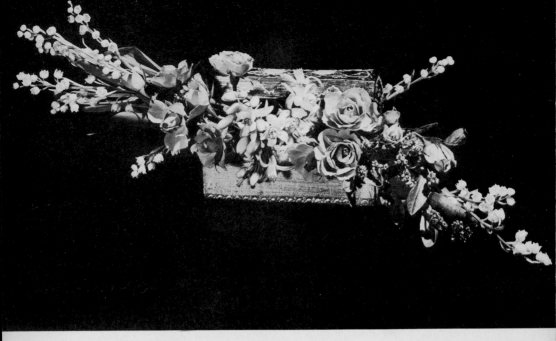

PLATE 76

A *little jewel box from Italy, hand-carved with satin finish of ivory and gold, is the container for this gift offering on a birthday or on Mother's Day. Tiny flowers spill from the half-closed lid: lilies of the valley and a few blades of their foliage, miniature roses of coral-pink, forget-me-nots on bare stems, and fragrant orange blossoms.*

138

valid (Plate 7). When it is possible to set the flowers in a container, they will be seen to much better advantage than when hurriedly arranged by a busy nurse.

BEREAVEMENT

To send a floral offering is a decorous observance of bereavement. White and delicate colors belong to infancy and childhood. Bright colors are suitable for a youth. Elderly people are sent rose, purple, white, or pastel tints. In other words the normal preferences of the age groups are observed. The so-called "set pieces," such as a wreath or a cross, are used more often for a person prominent in public life than for a relative or close friend.

Flowers may be sent to the home as well as to the chapel. Accompanied by an informal note, they now replace the call at the door which once was made.

CHAPTER VIII

Fruit and Vegetable Arrangements

T HE HISTORY of civilization can be traced through the development of art. As far back as we have any kind of record, man has voiced the needs of his body and the compulsion of his emotions in artistic expression. Drawing, painting, sculpture, poetry, the dance: the beginnings of all these forms of art are found in the seasonal aspects of man's domestic year. Symbolism and religious ritual celebrated the springtime of fertility and the ripening of the harvest. Of primitive man's art we have but the sketchiest remains. The prehistoric drawings in the caves of the Dordogne give outline representations of reindeer and ibex on pieces of bone. In Spain, in the cave of Santander, are three-color paintings of animals made, so it is said, at least fifty thousand years ago. These first expressions of bygone ages concern themselves entirely with animals because primitive man's vital contact came through the beasts with whom he disputed the earth.

As soon as man developed a medium of permanent record, he left us a legacy of nature expression. The most complete early record was made by the Egyptians, who not only sketched but preserved even the objects themselves in the dry air that filled the tombs of their dead. Paintings of funeral banquets show a combination of blossoms and fruit. Temple offerings composed of onions, figs, and grapes, their stems neatly tied with foliage, are pictured beside bunches of flowers. Paintings of banquet tables display baskets of vegetables and fruit—cucumbers, dates, melons, grapes—carefully segregated as to kind, never a miscellaneous assortment and never cluttered. With antiquity for support, it would be strange indeed if contemporary man made no artistic use of fruit and vegetables.

If you are hesitant before your first design in fruit or vegetables, you have only to call to mind the same principles that have always guided you in your work with flowers. You are still manipulating form, interesting textures, and beautiful coloring. It may help you to recall the manner in which early European artists utilized these plant growths. You have seen, perhaps, the "Virgin Enthroned" by Crivelli, where the Virgin is framed in a rich garland of apples and pears. Though this is a painting, you cannot help noticing the remarkable three-dimensional aspect of the fruit. The heaviness of form suggests a frame beautifully carved in wood. It is not surprising that the early Italian painters made rich use of fruit and vegetables, for the floral garland was first brought to perfection in Rome. The exquisite detail of overlapping leaves, of berries half-hidden, of nuts and fruit, of gently curving tendrils—all wrought in marble—is the first-century marvel of workmanship which Rome left to the world. The della Robbia family of Florence could not improve on the beauty of this sculpture of the Golden Age. Their pieces in New York's Metropolitan Museum of Art show their typical use of the garland. Figures surrounded by terracotta wreaths of fruit and foliage are wrought with the same beautiful sculptured effects created by the early Romans.

These great Florentine artists carried realism beyond the artistic portrayal of plant life. They correctly showed the association of fruits and vegetables and the animal life that belongs to plants. A design employing grapes, together with their leaves and tendrils, contains the sculptured form of a small tree frog frequently found on grape leaves. Another pattern made of the melon and the cucumber includes the lizard that lives in the fields where squash and melons grow. Like the sculptors of the Augustan Age, the della Robbias never combined a hodgepodge of vegetable or fruit forms, but limited the assortment to a specific grouping of forms or of kinds.

It is this matter of form that most distinctly separates fruit and vegetables from flowers. Even a relatively simple flower is a complex structure. The intricate fitting of the petals, the fineness of stamens and pistil, all must show if the blossom is to be appreciated properly. But vegetables and fruit fall easily into the broad classification of geometric figures. Many are round, such as the orange and the tomato; or oblate spheres, such as the turnip. Carrots approximate the cone; the flat sides of stalks of rhubarb or celery are extended rectangles; bananas and cucumbers are almost cylindrical. These shapes are firm and easy to handle. Moreover, their sharp outline provides the sculptured quality, the depth of three-dimensional form which is often very difficult to secure with delicate flowers.

Even the minor details have form—the "tail" of the beet and the radish, the surface planes of the banana which make for quick peeling, the crownlike calyx on the pomegranate, and the navel of the orange. Each one of these is boldly three-dimensional and can contribute to the total effect if you are working in abstract design (Plate 1).

With fruit and vegetables it is possible to create finished patterns quite unlike the conventional flower arrangements. Nevertheless, in making the design you employ the same principles that underlie your floral composition (Plate 77). First of all, your combination of materials must be harmonious. Usually it is better for the beginner to work with fruit or with vegetables, rather than to combine the two. The practical reason for this separation is that fruit decomposes much more quickly than vegetables. It is true that prize-winning designs have been created from an assembling of pineapple, peppers, gourds, onions, bananas, raspberries, strawberries, and eggplant; but nine times out of ten such a grouping will produce nothing better than a huddle of color and form. If such a design had been planned to express some appropriateness of season or occasion, it might be justified. Possibly it was arranged for Thanksgiving to symbolize the ripe fruitage of autumn. The intention might be permissible, but the particular selections could be questioned. The materials should belong to the country that produced the idea of Thanksgiving celebration. Pineapples and bananas could never be included, because they are exotics; nor the berries, since their season would be long past. Design is based on logical principles. Truly lovely effects have been achieved by experienced designers who have combined fruit and vegetables, but these artists are

PLATE 77

Six stalks of vivid red rhubarb make the diagonal placements. Green string beans establish the horizontal line, with each tip end pointing inward to return the eye to the two centered artichokes. Similarity of color in the beans and the artichokes and their related textures set against the smooth sheen of the rhubarb give this composition dramatic contrast in complementary color and textural differences.

143

PLATE 78

This plate shows a refined grouping of two varieties of squash. These two kinds were selected from the many members of the family because of the interesting contrast in their shape and texture. The nubbly skinned orange crookneck is strong in opposition to the yellow-green and the ivory-tinged disks of the summer squash with its smooth surface.

highly conscious of art principles and do not take unwarranted liberties with pattern or with nature.

Very interesting compositions can be created from a field narrowed to one species. You find almost unlimited variation of size, form, and texture among the squashes and in the citrus family (Plate 78). Before you attempt many designs with fruit and vegetables, you should investigate the Japanese morimono compositions. For centuries the Japanese have arranged fruits and vegetables in artistic patterns of masterly skill. They have a fine sense of the proper association of growing things. One design may be confined to the fruit of one species (Plate 79). Another may include cucumber and melon forms, or pineapples with bananas or other tropical fruit. The Japanese employ the same logic of selection as did the della Robbias of the Renaissance.

PRINCIPLES OF DESIGN

When you begin an arrangement of vegetables or fruit, you will remember that each shape has its particular function. Cylindrical forms are used for height; round and disk forms contribute weight to the axis. Any vegetable that combines two forms, as the turnip, will serve as a transitional step in the design. Very small vegetables such as radishes can be clustered for accent (Plate 80). The mass effect will be much like that of a single large vegetable, yet the multiplicity of single small forms, each with its own rounded contour, will provide variation. You may extend variation by other simple means. Do not, for example, use identical amounts of the different materials. Repetition becomes monotonous. Vary the size of the objects, some large, some small, some medium; but, again, do not use equal numbers of the differing sizes (Plate 81). From the available material select one kind, shape, size, texture, and color for dominance, just as you do in a flower arrangement; then use a relatively smaller number of the other kinds. An orderly placement of the subordinate forms will achieve transitions and rhythm through the pattern by preventing arrested vision or sudden leaps of the eye from spot to spot (Plate 82).

Scale is another consideration in design. After the size of the completed arrangement has been established, you must employ materials of suitable proportions. If you have planned a small pattern, you will substitute limes and fresh prunes for the more usual oranges and plums in order to reduce the composition to modest dimensions.

TEXTURE

You must remember that texture and form are of primary importance to the design, and determine the style. Heavy-textured vegetables such as the pumpkin are best suited for informal arrangement because of their weight and roughness. The glossy, thin-skinned pepper or tomato requires a more refined setting.

You think first of the skin alone, for the skin establishes the textural characteristics. You can create an artful design composed entirely of shiny-textured objects such as the eggplant and the green pepper. Another composition may need only a single detail of this highly reflective surface for accent. The range in textures is extensive, from the downy surface of the peach to the sheen of the apple, and from the nubbly, leathery-skinned avocado to the crisp leaf of lettuce.

Most vegetables convey a feeling of rough-textured casualness (Plate 83). Fruit offers a wide spread of delicacy and refinement. The luminous clearness of currants and gooseberries, the glimmer on lush, full bunches of grapes, and the powdered bloom on prunes and plums are lovely indeed in their response to light (Plate 66). This wide range of surface qualities makes it easy to contrive patterns of delicacy or of strength; to compose in formal or informal vein according to your inclination (Plate 84).

COLOR

Color combinations worked out in vegetable designs are frequently audacious; at first sight they may even seem incongru-

PLATE 79

The Japanese delight in picturing the life cycle of one plant. The fruit for this arrangement is the small tangerine. One branch holding bud, immature fruit, and fully ripened specimens is held in a pin-type holder under the pile of fruit. A few blossoms tucked among the tangerines complete the record of development. A typical Japanese slab of highly polished wood is the base for this Morimono composition.

147

PLATE 80

This grouping of vegetables displays the same principles of design as are used in floral arrangement. Cucumbers are set vertically like a spiked flower form to establish a height suited to the breadth of the wooden salad bowl. Two summer squash, through their indented edges and intermediate size, make a transition to the radishes clustered in a mass at the central axis. In a floral design small flower forms function as the radishes do here. The color harmony is complementary.

148

PLATE 81

This arrangement features interesting textural details. Rough bark, shading from gray to brown, makes the horizontal line. Ruggedly textured heads of asparagus form the vertical placement and fill the space to the bark. Summer squash roll their scalloped edges to the base of the asparagus and over the edge of the container. One squash at the far left emphasizes the heavy base.

149

PLATE 82

This is an excellent example of transition through the forms of the vegetables. Carefully developed transition is as conducive to rhythm in vegetable compositions as it is in flower or foliage arrangements when similar or opposing shapes are intermediately graded as to size and position. Celery stalks establish the triangular plan of the design. Cucumbers simulate shadow color as in a painting to emphasize contour lines and three-dimensional effects. They also fill the voids made by the celery and lead the eye to the tomatoes at the base. The round forms relieve vertical monotony and give a strong accent against the leaf tips of the celery. The highest tomato is impaled on a stick concealed by the feathery celery leaves.

PLATE 83

Broccoli and cauliflower are the dominant elements in this vegetable arrangement. The broccoli is tightly bunched to give the same shape as the cauliflower and to show similarity of texture. The sheen of the green-topped onions affords textural relief from the monotony of the rough heads. Although this design seems to be casual, as though the material had been picked from a vegetable stall and dumped into a basket, it is planned simplicity. It incorporates all the principles of art relating to monochromatic color, textured contrasts, form, and line. It achieves three-dimensional qualities by the adroit use of the dark and the light values.

PLATE 84

Two bunches of grapevine with their pendent clusters of fruit establish the design completed by individual grape leaves set in rosette at the axis. The container is a handmade vase of fine texture whose surface is brown with spatterings of light green glaze which seem like shadowed reflections of the suspended grapes.

152

ous. If you are confronted with a basket of purple onions and eggplant joined with yellow-orange tomatoes, you tell yourself that the tactile similarity of the thin, glossy skins unifies the composition. Or if you encounter red-violet cabbage, red tomatoes, and red-orange peppers, you discover that the heavy veining of the cabbage leaf and the tight lapping of its edges have established interesting contrast to the other vegetables in texture as well as in color.

To secure harmony and rhythm you regulate the color pattern with meticulous care. Vegetables are larger than blossoms and have firmly delineated contour lines. The color areas, therefore, are so pronounced and so sharply separated that easy, rhythmic movement is often difficult to attain. Because spottiness of hue is more distracting than isolated areas of differing texture, you work out the principles of color harmony, of contrasts and blends; and you secure your modulation by the same methods used to gain variation in size and form. The color problem is one reason why an arrangement of vegetables or fruit is sometimes more difficult than a similar design in flowers.

SELECTION AND PREPARATION

Experience in working with fruit and vegetables will enable you to determine the lasting quality of your specimens. A design intended to serve for several days should be made of materials still in the green stage or just beginning to show color. This is particularly true of berries and vegetables or fruit with stem attached (Plate 85). Otherwise they soon drop or break from the stem ends. If the articles of the design are later to be eaten, the fruit must be prime.

But whether or not they are to be eaten, both fruit and vegetables should be dust-free and otherwise as attractive as they can be made. Some kinds, as plum and grapes, when first picked are coated with a gray mist or bloom. To remove this powder by wiping and rubbing will reveal the true color of the fruit, but will at the same time destroy the lovely grayed effect which, perhaps, is preferable to the frequent harshness of unrelieved hue.

CONTAINERS

Containers for arrangements of fruit or vegetables are selected for their fitness with background and with the weight of the material. Plaques of wood, either crude or wrought with perfection of finish, are always suitable, as well as baskets, trays, and bowls. From the hand-hewn dough bowl of the pioneer to the sleek lacquer of the Oriental, all bowls have their use as receptacles for food plants. Put a rough, bold combination of vegetables on a wooden base or in heavy pottery or metal. Settle delicate sprays of currants and gooseberries with small clusters of grapes in a choice container of Oriental lacquer or teakwood. These dainty fruits go beautifully also in glass or silver or in any container of simple but elegant refinement.

Containers may be low or raised on stands like the European epergne or the compote. Use whatever height is most effective against the background (Plate 64).

COMBINATIONS

Flowers and foliage combine very successfully with fruit and vegetables. This use is logical, since without the blossom there would be no fruit. To link the bloom, the leaf, and the fruit of one species exemplifies the cycle of plant growth. It is the Japanese point of view (Plates 79, 85). Another approach combines the technique of the flower arranger and the purpose of the painter. If you group calendulas or sunflowers with pumpkins because of their similarity in color and form, you create a design that resembles a painting in still life.

You must remember two principles when you combine flowers of one species with fruit or vegetables of a different kind. First, bold flowers unite easily with rugged fruit and vegetables; delicate flowers harmonize with refined fruit and vegetables. Second, in any combination of fruit or vegetables with flowers and foliage, let one or the other preponderate. If the flowers are dominant, the fruit should be used as accent—and the reverse.

PLATE 85

Strawberries on a stand of Japanese lacquer depict the cycle of growth. The berries still cling to their stems. This composition is a Morimono in plan. It would be used by the Japanese as a way of presenting an edible fruit course as the conclusion of a meal.

155

CHAPTER IX

Holiday and Fete Day Arrangements

P LANT MATERIALS are the natural accompaniments of celebration. They add a festive note to occasions of rejoicing; they
can be quietly restrained with events of sober dignity. Because
our holidays are scattered through the year, many of them are
associated with seasonal plant growth.

NEW YEAR'S EVE AND DAY

The first holiday of the year is spiced with the lively tang of
evergreens. You can also make quite dashing arrangements of
dried materials that you have painted. The brilliance of colored
weeds and grasses is very smart when it appears against a background of pine and fir cuttings.

For the customary open house, use the earlier Christmas
decorations, but alter them sufficiently to suggest an entirely
different décor. You can accomplish this by eliminating some
arrangements and redoing others. Plate 86 shows a Christmas
mantel decoration of gilded leaves and green baubles. You can
retain the basic leaf structure, then replace the green balls with
brown pine cones. Thus with very little effort you will have a
mantel arrangement quite different in mood from the glitter of
the Christmas design. In Plate 87 sprays of fir, together with
ribbon bow and streamers used originally as exterior adornment

PLATE 86

Gilded aspidistra leaves make a glittering mantel for the holiday season. By reversing the design, the artist has provided an open space for a mirror or a painting. Had the vases been set at the two ends of the mantel rather than toward the center, they would have been transposed so that the lowest leaf would touch the mantel corner. In this plate the focal placement differs in the two designs: one uses pine cones; the other, baubles. When set in pairs the patterns must be of identical material, both made of pine cones or of ornaments.

PLATE 87

A copper-hued basket hangs from the beam of an exterior cornice, with long sprays of fir in diagonal sweep. The upper branch supports a clustering of agapanthus seed pods that have been coppered and dried, then finished with a topping of small yellow-green ornaments. Larger ornaments center the pattern, which is finished with a large bow and long streamers of green ribbon.

for the Christmas door, are now combined with a candle and ornaments. Entirely redesigned and set in a wire hanging-basket, this new pattern offers light and welcome hospitality to guests arriving on New Year's Eve. Plate 88 shows many sprays of evergreen material brightened by crisp red apples rubbed to a polish to provide a gay spot in a playroom.

The garden holds a meager floral display at this time of year. If the house decoration seems inadequate, make use of seasonal decorative details such as horns, bells, hats, noisemakers, white gloves, confetti, and the like. The ingenious floral artist can devise any number of ideas to supplement sparse floral display.

LINCOLN'S BIRTHDAY

On February 12 a patriotic floral theme will recall incidents linked with the life of Abraham Lincoln. If the scarcity of plant material limits your decoration, use accessories. A statue of Lincoln in a foreground of pine will express his youth and the vigor of his young manhood.

SAINT VALENTINE'S DAY

Appropriate to February 14 in the warm areas are early varieties of blossoming shrubs and trees. In cooler sections some shrubs and trees can be forced into early bloom or leafage (Plate 89). Forcing is accomplished by cutting a swelling branch, a foot or more in length, and placing it in water in a sunny area or a warm room in the house. It requires little attention other than the recutting of the stem from time to time to keep the immersed end of the branch open. If the stalk clogs, it will not take up water freely. A few of the more readily forced plant materials are almond, apple, apricot, azalea, cherry, Chinese magnolia, crab apple, flowering quince, forsythia, horse chestnut, peach, pear, plum, poplar, and pussy willow.

The daintiness of forced leafage or fruit blossoms will give a delicate interpretation to St. Valentine's Day (Plate 90). A container with a pedestaled Cupid base or a heart motif will seem as choice as the sentiment it expresses if arranged with a spare amount of florist material, such as the lily of the valley or miniature roses. The heaviness of a profuse arrangement would belie the sincerity of youthful affection. Be ingenious; for a composition, however novel, will please if it is small and pretty (Plate 91).

WASHINGTON'S BIRTHDAY

February 22 suggests another patriotic theme. Perhaps flowers in red, white, and blue are not available. Then combine flags, other symbolic forms, or tri-colored ribbon supplemented by flowers of one color, preferably white. If you have forced or natural tree bloom, you can select an incident connected with the life of Washington and give it humorous treatment in a floral design (Plate 92).

SAINT PATRICK'S DAY

March 17, once a holiday of Irish settlers, has been adopted by all America. Green, symbolic of the day, heralds the coming of spring with its lively floral display. The tiny shamrock is so inconspicuous that its small, three-petaled leaf does not lend itself effectively to an arrangement. Here you can again be imaginative by employing such accessories as green ribbon, larger replicas of shamrocks, potatoes combined with foliage— and, as accessory, white clay pipes or an Irish harp. The Molucca balm, an old European favorite now renamed bells of Ireland, is very appropriate in color. Under its new name it fits handsomely any St. Patrick's Day design, though neither the Irish Americans nor their ancestors attached any significance to it (Plate 93). Green garden foliage, employed with white flowers, make a suitable composition.

There are few plants with blossoms of natural green. You can produce green flowers artificially if you want them for decora-

PLATE 88

A tree structure has been built from many small cuttings of
Japanese yew. Red apples caught on sticks emphasize the alternating
rhythm of the yew sprays, left to right, over and over again, from the
base to the tip. An old tree stump is the ground support. One apple
resting on the stump seems to have fallen from its place in the branches.
This design illustrates how an arrangement originally constructed for
Christmas can be modified for New Year's Day.

PLATE 89

Forked sprays of pussy willow, one upright and one pendent, are set in the long placements of the design. Soulangeana magnolia is used for the beautiful center. One blossom has been forced open to serve as focal interest and to repeat the rounded detail of the container. The brown of the willow stems and the container is subtly relieved by the delicate shadings of the magnolia hues.

PLATE 90

Apricot sprays forced into early bloom curve gently as if bent by the spring breeze. Rosettes of an early flowering pittosporum repeat the form of the wheels and the arching backs of the bisque carts. The presence of the tiny Cupids makes this a charming arrangement for a gift on St. Valentine's Day.

PLATE 91

Elaborate designs can be fabricated from commonplace material. For this pattern a wire coat hanger was inverted and bent into heart shape. It was then covered with bits of dried maidenhair fern that had previously been bleached and tinted pink. Each little spray of fern was fastened to the frame with transparent adhesive tape. Sprays of pink flowering plum at the sides of the heart and clusters of large almond blossoms at the center of the base complete the composition.

164

PLATE 92

An old tree stump, presumably from the orchard, and the ax tell
the story from which this design was made. Crab apple blossoms, which
can easily be forced into bloom, are held in a pin-type holder concealed
behind the stump.

PLATE 93

The clear green of the bells of Ireland is intensified by the cane grass. The white and green stripings of the grass at the middle of the arrangement not only strengthen the color pattern of the floral material, but also increase the depth of the composition.

tion. It is a simple matter to color white flowers. First allow them to wilt. When they are noticeably limp, cut the stem end of the flowers and place them in green ink, either at full strength or slightly diluted. The flower stems suck up the fluid very rapidly and soon the green is apparent in the bloom.

White or green containers of glass or pottery are most suitable for this occasion.

EASTER

Easter is never a set date. It may fall on any Sunday in the thirty-five day period between March 21 and April 26, as determined by the conjunction of the spring equinox and the succeeding full moon. When this holiday arrives in mid or late April, the soil has had enough time to warm up, so that spring flowers will appear even in the cool regions. In southern United States the Easter lily is in full bloom in outdoor gardens, along with azaleas and other choice spring blooms (Plate 16).

The holiness of the day quite naturally is expressed by the use of white flowers (Plate 3). You need not feel limited to white, however, since your garden is filled with the gentle colors of spring from the pale gold of the daffodil to the fairness of the violet hyacinth. Whether your arrangement is large or small, you should strive for simplicity and restraint. Spiritual aspiration is in no way dependent on size (Plate 94). If you include accessories when the theme of the arrangement is religious, select them with extreme caution (Plate 95).

Easter morning is also associated with the gaiety of children's laughter. The Easter egg baskets, the baby chick, the duckling, and the little rabbit are now a part of the holiday. All these find ready interpretation in novelty floral designs (Plates 22, 96).

MAY DAY

The world has always celebrated the opening of May because May Day signifies the coming of warmth and sunshine. Centuries ago the solemn Romans paid tribute to Flora, the goddess of spring and flowers. Down through the ages the maidens of England in gay-sprigged gowns have danced their light-hearted measures on the village green. The first day of May has been set aside to exalt the beauty of nature and the joy of the spirit as expressed by youthful whirlings of the dance (Plate 97).

A tiny Maypole makes an attractive centerpiece for the dining-table. Charming, too, as well as traditional, is the May Day basket for table adornment or a gift to intimate friends. Hang it on the door filled with bunches of delicate flowers (Plate 98). A basket of glass or woven reeds with handles is the appropriate container. The flowers should seem to have come from your garden. Primroses, pansies, violets, forget-me-nots, mignonette, miniature roses, and other sweet-scented flowers are lovely gathered in small bunches.

MOTHER'S DAY

Since the recent introduction of Mother's Day, the second Sunday in May has become an established holiday. It can be the occasion for presenting to Mother a gift of lasting value or a floral offering of simple beauty (Plate 76). The arrangement should be quietly dignified, made of her favorite blossoms. Some older women enjoy an arrangement composed of many floral varieties reminiscent of happy experiences. If such a profuse collection demands a massed design, it must not seem heavy or stuffed. A loose, unstereotyped arrangement will express more sincere emotion than an intricate design.

For the youthful or sophisticated mother the arrangement may be small. The flowers probably will be the orchid, the camellia, the gardenia, the lily of the valley, or any flower with an air of distinction.

MEMORIAL DAY

Although Memorial Day was originated for military observance, the custom of placing flowers on military graves has broad-

PLATE 94

Blossoms of the calla lily in differing stages of development have been selected for their harmony with this modern figure of the Madonna. The spathes of the open lilies repeat the oval sweep of the petal forms that are a part of the base of the little statue. The Madonna of the Flowers was designed and named by the author and modeled to his specifications by a noted English artist.

169

PLATE 95

This exquisite design pictures all the reverence and the sanctity of Easter morning. Orange blossoms and leaves are set at the base of valley lilies and their foliage, with a small spray of maidenhair fern. The figures of two tiny angels complete the arrangement.

PLATE 96

Sprays of pussy willow set as one placement simulate a small
tree, with bright-hued daffodils that appear to be growing at the base.
Yellow pottery ducklings rest among the rocks. The composition is
delightfully fresh with the outdoor crispness of the spring season.

PLATE 97

The container for this delicate miniature is a hand-painted porcelain powder box. The placements of valley lilies from the tip of the tallest stem to the lowest flower at the bottom are worked out in successively shortened lines to provide a gay, swirling rhythm. Heads of allium outline and fairly well cover the powder-box lid. The little Dresden dancer fingering the tip of a lily is poised as if waiting her cue in a springtime ballet.

PLATE 98

Here is a charmingly sentimental arrangement for May Day. The little reed basket holds an assortment of old-fashioned flowers: pansies, Queen Anne's lace, and fragrant mignonette. The bow and streamers of yellow ribbon add a special touch of modern elegance to the gift.

PLATE 99

The firecracker was made from red cardboard with an open space left in the center to hold a container. Flower placements are set in a diagonal line in keeping with the spirit of the holiday. Sprays of white stock and blue cornflowers hold a few heads of bright red carnations in the center that are topped by a band of actual firecrackers. The long fuse and the box of matches add sufficient realism to the floral decoration.

174

ened to include all the dead. Patriotic dignity prescribes offerings to the war dead. Stylized wreaths of green magnolia leaves or bronzed palm sprays are beautiful, yet simple. Arrangements of red, white, and blue flowers, or a composition of any one of these hues is effective. Garden flowers clustered naturally seem more suitable for the non-military dead. Peonies, roses, lilies, and gladioli are seasonal blossoms.

INDEPENDENCE DAY

For the Fourth of July the colors of red, white, and blue can be worked into highly dramatic designs. Although July is one of the warm months, the garden is normally filled with a profusion of flowers. Should excessive heat destroy the beauty of floral growth, use accessories. The flag, stars, patriotic figurines, or even firecrackers may suggest an idea for a theme or a container (Plate 99). White garden flowers are: geranium, stock, delphinium, larkspur, gladiolus, and carnation; red blossoms: geranium, salvia, carnation, and gladiolus; blue flowers: cornflower, lupine, and delphinium.

LABOR DAY

The first Monday in September is usually warm. Since it is a day for outdoor entertaining, plan an arrangement for the barbecue or the picnic area which will withstand the sun. A design of foliage with some floral accent is safest. Containers will be in keeping with outdoor environment. Low bowls broad enough to afford a clear view of the water look cool.

HALLOWEEN

The last day of October is the time for carnival and goblins. The most suitable colors are, of course, orange and black.

Orange is symbolic of the fires used in ancient times to frighten away ghosts, and black hints of witches and the mystery of night. Pumpkins and black masks are traditional accessories, along with broomsticks, black cats, bats, and witches; and the iron cauldron is an appropriate container. If you have given your garden seasonal maintenance, you will have marigolds, dahlias, and chrysanthemums from pale yellow to deep orange. Wild sunflowers and black-eyed Susans still linger by the roadside in some sections of the country.

THANKSGIVING

The fourth Thursday in November honors harvest time and gives spiritual acknowledgment for the abundance of nature. The period of fruiting is over; the cycle of the seasons is being completed.

Emphasize the harvest motif with floral, vegetable, or fruit treatment. Your first idea, perhaps, is an abundant design. Better than heavy massing, however, is a pattern that suggests rather than exemplifies the plentitude of well-stocked store-houses. Pendent clusters of grapes with a few sprays of their own foliage give more aesthetic pleasure than an overly massed combination of many varieties of fruit and vegetables. Any grouping of several kinds must be done with circumspection. Only through severe simplicity of line pattern can you achieve distinction with lavish material (Plate 21). Any flowers combined with fruit or vegetables must be in seasonal and regional harmony with the food plants. Imported exotics, though always available and always attractive in themselves, destroy the idea for which the holiday was created.

The hues of autumn are traditionally red and yellow; nevertheless, Thanksgiving arrangements may be varied in color. If you are selective in your search, you will find many plant materials appropriate to your purpose. Burgundy-red celosia combined with purple or black grapes are rich enough for any taste. The intense purples of eggplant, onions, and cabbage make a splendidly opulent monochromatic harmony.

For too many people Thanksgiving is a highly material feast

day; and an arrangement has only one possibility, something after the idea of a centerpiece. But the holiday carries spiritual connotation with obligations extending far beyond the consuming of an elaborate dinner. Far better. than one table arrangement seen only briefly would be designs throughout the house.

The entry door or hall should express a gracious welcome (Plate 78). Festoon the mantel of library or living-room, or group fruit and foliage upon it. (Plate 100). If you have little variety in materials, extend one floral theme throughout the house. You can vary the designs to avoid monotony and to provide a pattern suitable for each location. But through the recurrence of color and plant materials you will ensure a decorative unity that can culminate in the table arrangement if you wish (Plate 101).

Containers can be suggested by the plant material or selected to conform with the holiday. The cornucopia, symbol of plenty, is suitable for any public type of decoration and for gatherings larger than an intimate family group. You will prefer for your own home the familiar containers that are graceful accompaniments to the background and the furnishings of your house. Such receptacles as the compote, the epergne, ironstone tureens or platters, choice wooden plaques or trays, mats, objects of brass or iron are all suited to the Thanksgiving theme, even in its most limited sense.

If you depend upon your flower border for the material of your arrangements, you must have plan and plant well in advance of the Thanksgiving season. You will want chrysanthemums in differing sizes and colors, as well as the comb and the plume celosia in red and gold. Marigolds and zinnias come in rich autumn hues. The berried shrubs will be in full color.

CHRISTMAS

In planning for Christmas you should select a pattern of adornment. If you wish to illustrate spiritual meanings, use religious symbols, such as angels, stars, candles, or a crèche. If you stress the gaiety and the merrymaking, you will need pine and fir. Both evergreens are easy to obtain. They can be dressed with unaffected simplicity or given a highly stylized treatment to accord with the most sophisticated modern interior. The entrance to the grounds or the door of the home establishes the pattern to recur throughout the house. The green of conifer with red ornamentation is used here for the exterior treatment as a symbol of hospitality (Plate 102). The evergreen theme is used again, this time in a container because the poinsettias that have been combined with the evergreens require water. This arrangement will be set in the hall or in an adjoining room (Plate 103). The Christmas tree, traditional in green and red, occupies an important position in the main room. Placed as it is against a background of corner windows, it unites the jocund warmth of the interior and the crisp chill of the outdoors (Plate 104).

Americans delight in glimmering color and metallic luster. For this one last week of the year we deck our rooms with shining balls, then regale our tired nerves with the color of the tiny lights that glint from every arching surface. When the house has an interior of elegant simplicity, you can gain some of this sparkle from treated plant-cuttings. You can achieve extraordinary beauty by either silvering, gilding, or coppering plant foliage or entire branches. At the entryway of this home use a black iron container holding a diagonal placement of silvered weed stalks that support yellow-green baubles. Place this design in a niche in the hall or hang it outside the door as a lighting fixture. For this latter setting remove the tallest central stalk to provide room for a candle in the center of the container (Plate 105). The following is a typical Christmas decoration in the home. The living-room, with its silvered gray walls and black accents in the furniture, has three displays: a fireplace decoration, a candle, and a tree. The fireplace façade is a shining copper band against a coral background. Two vertical arrangements set in recessed niches in supporting columns are of coppered leaves and coral-hued ornaments (Plate 106). A coral candle is embellished with coppered plant material (Plate 107). The ingeniously beautiful tree is placed against the wall. The banana stalk and the basal leaves, all of them silvered, build the main lines of the pattern. They give strength and stability to the design which without them would be too frail in form to support its luster. The branches are fashioned of luminous wands

PLATE 100

A stylish mantel trim for Thanksgiving is made of dark green foliage. Two aspidistra leaves establish the line in each arrangement. Magnolia leaves for the principal portion of the diagonal bands have been wired and assembled in the manner described in Plate 70. Italian limes are similarly clustered to depict the importance of fruit and foliage for this holiday.

179

PLATE 101

Select a dozen or more tip ends of magnolia branches for the
assembling of this simulated tree. The height of the tree will be determined by the length of the longest branch. Center this cutting in a
pin-type holder; then work downward, filling in on all sides with
gradually shortened sprays until the design resembles a pyramidal tree.
Place loose leaves at the base to conceal the holder. The orange limes
are wired as described in Plate 70 and centered in the rosette of each
branch. Since the container holds water and all the sprays are held in
the holder, the design will last for weeks. The fruit must be replaced
every seven or eight days.

PLATE 102

An espalier effect in fir is made by cutting from a small tree all the branches that grow at the back and directly toward the front. This pruning retains the branches that grow out to the sides. The ornamental topping is made of small green beads strung in lengths. The midrib is heavily decorated with two sizes of ornaments, the larger ones set to suggest a zigzag pattern down the trunk. Green satin ribbon of the same hue as the baubles at the top makes the wide diagonal spread across the gate, finished with generous bows.

181

PLATE 103

A very small tree has been pruned in the manner described in *Plate* 102. A garland of furled silver foil spirals down from the star at the top of the tree. Vivid red poinsettias have been defoliated, then completely immersed in water until crisp. Arranged in a triangle, they alternate with the brilliant star ornaments to multiply the gay effect for the holiday.

182

PLATE 104

Before decorating a Christmas tree, equalize the length of the spreading horizontal branches by clipping. Also secure equal distance between the layers of branches. This is accomplished by lifting a sagging branch and fastening it by a suspended wire to the branch above. Prune out any branches that obviously interfere with the purity of strong, straight lines. Mass the heavy ornaments along the main stalk. Place the smaller ornaments at the tips of the branches. This traditional tree in red and green ornamentation is smartly stylized by the inclusion of ribbon bows and puckered streamers in spruce green.

PLATE 105

    The spreading design is made of loosely fingered umbels of wild grass clipped short to increase the strength of the leaf blade. After it has been dried and painted silver, small colored ornaments can be inserted at the tip ends of the blades. Larger ornaments, centered near the base of the design, are held in the crotch formed by the blades.

PLATE 106

Two similar placements of coppered aspidistra leaves in vertical treatment conform with the severity of the matched columns of the fireplace. The end caps on the ornaments have been removed so that each bauble can be supported by a short stick. Furled leaves adjacent to the ornaments conceal the pin-type holders used in assembling the design. The aspidistra leaves do not require water and, when painted, will last indefinitely.

PLATE 107

Tall dried umbels of agapanthus that have been given a burnished copper tone hold glittering green bead ornaments on each
spike. The large yule candle is a vivid coral color. Coppered magnolia
leaves add a flourish to this simple, yet brilliant, composition. The
container is gray with splashes of coral on a shiny glaze.

186

of plastic bristles that have been dipped in coral dye. Maidenhair fern that has been bleached, then dyed coral, gives strong color accent to the silver trunk. The daintiness of the material, together with the deftness of its assembling, has effected a delicacy quite unusual for its six-foot length (Plate 108).

The employment of metallics on plant growth is an American inspiration. With such glittering material it is possible to achieve a brilliance of style that for sheer artistic expression is unmatched.

PLATE 108

 The source of this material is a banana tree from which the long bladed leaves have been removed and the barren stalk painted silver. Nylon fishing cord dyed coral is clustered and wired in tassels to a long pointed stick. The banana is so porous that the sharpened sticks are easily placed in pyramidal pattern. Silvered aspidistra leaves broaden and give stability to the base. Four large nylon stars of abstract pattern follow a center path. Maidenhair fern that has been bleached, tinted coral, and then dried is fastened to the tree. Clear glass Christmas ornaments grouped in a mesh of silvered strands rest at the base surrounded by silvered leaves.

188

CHAPTER X

Centerpiece Design

THERE IS NO fundamental difference between a centerpiece design and the usual flower arrangement. If a design is really good, it can be adapted to almost any location, provided you keep in mind the point of view of the observer. Since a centerpiece is intended to be attractive from all sides and any angle of vision, it must be so completed that its beauty will be apparent at first view from above, before the guest is seated, and then from whatever place at table he may occupy.

If the table is small, you should choose a low, flat design so that the general conversation can be carried on without any difficulty of obscured vision (Plate 12). The term "centerpiece," however, implies a more ceremonial gathering than the two or three guests of a family party. The table is enlarged to such an extent that a single low piece would be dwarfed by the size of its setting and the importance of the occasion. The customary floral arrangement for such a table is symmetrical (Plate 109).

Consistency of tone is the most important characteristic of table design. Some one feature must be chosen to dominate the harmony and everything else keyed to this detail. The color pattern presents the chief difficulty. Usually the color is determined by the china. If the design on the service plates is a solid color, the problem is simple. Should the design comprise more than one color, select one of the hues and choose all other appointments with reference to this tone. Choose the cloth, the accessories, and the flowers to match, to contrast, or to harmonize with the color selected from the china.

Though no table fabric is richer or more beautiful than exquisite white damask, the tastes of the twentieth century permit, even encourage, the use of a colored cloth. Damask is very expensive, the colored as well as the white. Beautifully rich effects are now available in the modern synthetic fabrics with a sheen reminiscent of damask and colors as soft and delicate or as bold as you desire. Such a cloth is correct at the formal table, provided you select the color with reason. The conventional choice is a pastel, but special occasions can fire your imagination to the creation of spectacular effects. A cloth of maroon or purple may be unusual, but the taste of today sanctions departures from tradition. With a cloth of rich purple rayon use a service of cobalt-blue dishes, amethyst glass, and flatware of old silver. Or spread a wine-red cloth with flatware of gold alloy, dishes banded in gold, and stemware of cranberry glass.

Modern formality has liberalized table-settings to permit the use of many fabrics other than damask. Handsome lace and embroidery are more rare than damask, more difficult to obtain, but either makes a superb foundation. Both lace and damask are exceedingly dignified, in exact accord with a room of traditional appointments. Other fabrics can be used for formal dinners if you wish a feeling of lightness or daintiness. Many fine-textured materials are wholly charming with delicate china and thin glass or crystal. You can create sparkle and brilliance with organdy, both the silk and the cotton thread. No fabric is quite so crisp as organdy, so firmly airy. It comes in white or pastel hues; it is either plain or worked with fastidiously refined embroidery stitches or hand-painted. White organdy or fine net spread above an undercloth of satin gives an astonishingly beautiful effect, delicate yet rich.

The colors of the centerpiece design will be chosen in the same way and for the same reasons that established the color of the cloth. The hue of the container is determined by any one of several items of the table service. If the container is silver, it will seem to be an extension of the flatware. Silver is good on any occasion, either formal or informal, wherever silver flatware is used (Plate 110). A crystal container is suitable with glassware of the same color (Plate 111), or a white container if the china is dominantly white.

If you live in an apartment with limited storage space, choose a few good containers of inconspicuous form and color that will

PLATE 109

Sprays of the bells of Ireland, with a few clusters of tiny grapes and grape leaves, are the fresh materials of this arrangement which has been prepared for a traditional formal setting. The elegance essential to the occasion is gained through the use of accessories. The designer has achieved richness by placing the design in an alabaster urn and employing branches of alabaster grapes to provide a shining luminosity near the table.

191

PLATE 110

The floral design for this informal dinner uses powder-pink stock and heads of pink hydrangeas. The conventionalized horizontal plan has been varied by the opposing diagonals of six pink carnations. The container is silver, the cloth pale pink, and the china gray with silver banding. The delicacy and grace of the plant material and the accessories lend distinction to the setting.

192

PLATE 111

The contemporary home uses handsome glass and plant material in keeping with the plainness of its architectural lines. This formal dinner-setting of black glass is exceedingly simple. Black strelitzia nicolai dignifies a setting that stresses textural quality and arresting form.

be appropriate for any function. In the selection of these containers, observe one very important principle: harmony. These containers must be in mood or key with all the table appointments. If the china is very colorful, with conspicuous pattern in the decoration, the glass should be plain and the silver very simple, in both line and ornamentation. If the silver is so richly embossed that it is the most elaborate feature of the setting, the china and the glass should be plain. Perhaps the cloth sets the standard of elegance. If you want the cloth to be noticed above everything else, let the glass, the china, and the silver be inconspicuous. In other words, the principles of design apply to table appointments as to any other artistic expression, and only one feature can be dominant. You can select your few containers, therefore, of silver, glass, and porcelain. But choose receptacles of such plain lines and spare ornamentation that they will harmonize with all your other appointments and will not attract much attention to themselves.

If the occasion is less formal than the dinner dominated by damask or lace, the color possibilities are even greater. The color plan can be extended to include an additional tone in the service. Colored glassware can be substituted for clear crystal. The flower container can match the glass or the service plate or the cloth. Ponderous containers of heavy material are seldom used because they do not harmonize with the delicacy of table appointments.

The centerpiece is usually round, triangular, or horizontal. If the table is round or oval, a rounded design continues the shape established by the cloth. If the table is rectangular and long, a triangular or horizontal composition is preferable. A tall, slender vertical might suggest the length of the cloth, but would be too wandlike and thin to be attractive. The design should not be massive—it would seem overpowering; also it would block the vision across the table. One of the advantages of the triangular design is the symmetrical narrowing toward the top, with its necessary voids. If the table is very long, or if it seems desirable to use a small arrangement, a garland can extend the floral effect.

The color scheme of the arrangement must be simple. If the cloth is pale and the dinner service delicate, the flowers should be pastels. A monochromatic design with several values of one color is correct, or a pattern of one color supplemented with white. Less formal, but very interesting designs can be made with a combination of several pastel colors.

When you use artificial light, you must investigate the lighting equipment of the room. If the light source is the so-called "daylight lamp," or "blue light," the color value of the flowers will be approximately true, as if viewed in the daytime; but if older-type lamps are used, the values of certain colors will be changed. Blues and violets will fade out to a rather nondescript gray. The entire red scale, from deep tones to pale pink, will remain true, even in the older light. If you want to use blue and violet in the decorative scheme, it is usually a very simple matter to replace ordinary lamps with daylight lamps.

You can make good use of candles with artificial light. Beautiful candlesticks of modest design, if placed with care, enhance the decoration of the table. White candles have always been suitable for formal occasions. But if the cloth is colored, the candles can match the cloth or the china.

If you have place mats instead of a cloth for luncheon or dinner, the same principles of centerpiece design prevail. For because these place sets will be of the same degree of elegance and formality as the cloth they replace, they will require floral adornment of corresponding quality (Plate 112).

The informal luncheon is a gay affair. Because it is almost always an entirely feminine gathering, it is invariably dainty. Everything on the table must be pretty (Plate 113). Any fabric is suitable for a table-covering. But a damask cloth is perhaps too severe for a luncheon mood. Lace, of course, is lovely, or organdy in either cloth or place mats. Fine linen place mats of the handkerchief-linen quality or the heavier, hand-woven effect can be hemstitched or embroidered lightly with small motifs. Colored voile is dainty; both net and marquisette, cotton or silk thread, are exquisite on the bare table or over a colored undercloth or mat. Both of these gossamer fabrics become quite elegant with a bit of hand-sewing. Silk net and silk marquisette stitched with colored silk thread or metallic thread of silver or gold are choice. The metallic threads are very lovely when applied to colored marquisette.

A table-setting of such simple beauty is the ideal foundation for a service of figured china, preferably a small floral pattern,

PLATE 112

    This triangular design was planned for a formal dinner with place mats instead of the full cloth. The mats are imported ecru lace. Quilled ecru chrysanthemums are combined with bleached barley heads, crab apples, and small magnolia leaves. Whenever a low container is used for the floral decoration of a formal occasion, it is not only proper but imperative that the vertical element be tall. Its height must be narrow so that it is not a visual obstacle across the table. When this principle is applied, as in this design, the table-setting has great dignity.

196

PLATE 113

A horizontal line for the floral pattern of a luncheon is highly desirable. The container need not be flat on the table. Slightly raised, it displays airiness and grace. The plant material includes oleanders, carnations, miniature roses, and a few gardenias for their fragrance. The colors of both flowers and accessories make a quiet blend of yellow, white, silver, and gray.

PLATE 114

For this delightful brunch table an antique coffee grinder is used for its novelty as well as for its contribution to the artistic plan of the design. Its drawer has been pulled out to support the figs and other fruit. Behind the grinder the concealed pin-type holder supports a sturdy branch of ripe peaches, a few yellow chrysanthemums, apples, and grapes. The complete arrangement is noticeable for the dominance of red, blue, and yellow hues.

with colored glassware to match the flowers on the dishes. A low floral arrangement with quaint figurines will complete the table.

A luncheon table such as any of these is beautiful enough for any of the special occasions dear to the feminine heart. Announcements, showers, birthdays, anticipated vacation trips, return from travel—all of these provide gay opportunity for a festive luncheon. The specific reason for the event can be indicated by place cards or figurines, or an announcement device at each plate.

Much less elegant than these carefully worked out luncheons is the casual gathering of friends for lunch or breakfast (Plate 114). The friendliness and informality of these affairs forbids the use of conservative appointments. If the season permits, set the table outdoors on the porch or the terrace. The cloth may be as colorful as you desire. Gingham, heavy linen, crash, Indianhead, sail cloth—the list of fabrics is as extensive as the shelves of your best department store can supply.

Novelty mats of reed or raffia or grass, of heavy, crocheted carpet warp or plastic or cork, have a pronounced textural effect that is always interesting. Severely tailored mats of figured linen or crash, or hemstitched pieces, give a crisp smartness to the place-setting. If the mats are of solid color, napkins in complementary hue, or in deeper values of the same hue, are good-looking.

The dishes will be as informal as the setting—pottery or very gay china. And the informal flower arrangement, set in an informal container, will match or complement the dishes (Plate 115).

The modern hostess uses centerpiece design for occasions other than meals. Afternoon tea is as carefully planned and as elegant as a formal dinner (Plate 116). The long table, either in the dining-room or at one end of the living-room, wears a handsome cloth. Often it is lace. More interesting, perhaps because less frequently seen, is the cloth of sheer fabric over color. White net or organdy over green provides a cool tone for the warmest days; over gold, it suggests the ripeness of autumn; over silver, it evinces the crispness of spring or the frost of a winter night, lovely for a Christmas tea. There is usually room at a tea for a rather large flower arrangement. The design may be tall, since the guests are standing and are generally on only one side of the table. It must be made of choice flowers in a refined pattern, then set in an elegant container (Plate 117).

While the ritual of the tea is so completely established by precedent that it is difficult to err, the buffet meal presents an altogether different problem (Plate 118). The buffet is the least-stereotyped meal you can serve, and one that requires the most careful planning. It may be, in fact often is, highly informal; but it never can be casual, like a breakfast. It is always gay. It can be served at any time of day, from early morning to midnight. If the occasion is a dinner or a luncheon in a dining-room of conservative furnishings, the buffet table will be set with fine china and silver serving dishes. Informal pottery, large chop plates, handsome metal cooking-dishes that can be moved from the kitchen to most buffet tables, will not go with Sheraton furniture and crystal chandeliers. If the table is large, the flower arrangement often may be imposing. It can, of course, be tall, since the guests do not sit at the table. If the food occupies most of the space, set the flowers at one end of the table, or at one side if the table is pushed against the wall. These positions make an asymmetric design possible which you can balance by a large object of table service. The important thing in placing the arrangement is to have it where its beauty will complete the design of the table-setting but not obstruct the service as the guests wait upon themselves.

The small modern house of the average housewife is much less formal than the houses of even a decade ago. The emphasis today is placed on the kitchen and the game or family room. Much of the time at home is spent in these areas. Most kitchens are arranged for informal family meals, even of the not-too-casual type. Usually a space is designed specifically for eating. There may be a dinette, or dining-nook, or a spot equipped with a small table or sometimes with a shelf that pulls down for the meal and at other times is folded against the wall. Perhaps a counter is close to the cooking-area, in a location that makes for ease and speed of service. These kitchens are a delight to the eye, with their beautiful and sometimes spectacular color schemes. Flowers are a natural accompaniment to a kitchen done in color (Plate 65). The appointments and accessories—the curtains, the towels, the cloths, the canisters, the dishes, the

PLATE 115

Informal roadside beauty is simply portrayed in an arrangement for the breakfast table. Sprays of dried barley harmonize in texture as well as in hue with the reed-basket container and the place mats. The wild sunflowers, the dock, and the cattails are in the same tones as the Mexican dishes of hand-wrought pottery.

201

PLATE 116

The floral pattern for a tea requires less attention to height and studied voids than the arrangement prepared for an occasion when the guests are seated. Gladioli, always available and economical to buy, if not grown at home, establish the height and a stability desirable with the weight of the heavy Waterford glass compote. Long branches of white oleander extend horizontally, with clustered heads of the same flower recessed and centered at the lip of the container.

PLATE 117

An elaborate Venetian glass epergne holds an unusual design of fruit and flowers. The materials are clusters of grapes, grape leaves, and the ivory-hued star-of-Bethlehem. At the base of the container a spray of green persimmons rests on the ivory cloth. This style of container provides the necessary height and proportions for entertaining on the grand scale, or for special occasions such as a wedding party, a banquet, or a reception.

PLATE 118

This buffet design expresses autumn richness. Warm-toned chrysanthemums and orange kniphofia are dramatized by the use of the exciting diagonal line. The pomegranate branch resting on the table and its fruit grouped in the brown container stabilize the diagonal thrust. The container in mat glaze is an original by the author.

204

flowers—are worked out with as much fidelity to color harmony as was the dining-room service.

Besides being very lovely, these kitchens are slick and modern, warm and inviting for a quick breakfast or a pick-up supper. A kitchen may be finished in birch, with cupboard doors and a counter softly waxed which gleam in the light and are smooth to the touch. The curtains may be bright red-orange, the napkins red-orange to match. Place mats of turquoise hold a breakfast service of turquoise pottery. At one end of the counter we might see a basket of rolls and a coffee percolator of red-orange enamel; at the other end another basket, filled with fruit—bananas, persimmons, and oranges.

A delightful breakfast for St. Valentine's Day or Easter, for May Day or any other festive springtime day, can be set on a dinette table. Use place mats of any modern, inexpensive fabric—cotton broadcloth, gingham, or the more-elegant cotton satin. Set a few flowers in a low-footed goblet to complete the gay note.

If you live in an apartment in town, high above the city streets, you can create the similitude of a garden. Almost every kitchen has the workbench under a window. Trim the windows with curtains of sheer material and set a row of small bowls at the back of the bench against the window. Select a flower in two colors that fit the kitchen trim, arranging the two colors in alternate order in the bowls to give the illusion of a row of flowers growing outside the window. In hot weather substitute foliage plants or ferns with a few bright flowers set upright as if growing, or use planters.

CHAPTER XI

Floral Containers

IF YOU ARE AN average flower arranger, you have an assortment of containers. A well-stocked cabinet will display a variety of sizes and shapes in glass, china, ceramics, and metals. If you are the acquisitive type, eager to enlarge your collection from the perennial supply of novelties, you should choose cautiously from the tempting array. You seek in a container the same qualities embodied in your floral arrangements: design, color, and texture. Any good container will be pleasing in form, with finely molded contours of clean line and attractive proportion. The material of which it is made is relatively unimportant; the basic form is the first consideration.

The choicest containers are of a distinguished simplicity. Vertical and horizontal; circular, oval, rectangular: these elemental geometric terms describe the primary characteristics of excellent form. Only when these forms are combined do you encounter difficulties, when curves are slapped upon the straight line, when the vertical is so robust as to infringe upon the horizontal. In any combination or variation of line and form, the silhouette must still exhibit the fine purity of contour which is characteristic of the simple basic form.

An object can be very beautiful and yet be unsuitable as a container. Perhaps it is so unusual in form as to be wholly arresting; then the observer, caught in his wonder or curiosity at the shape, will not even see the flowers set within. Perhaps it is overly ornate with sumptuous richness of decoration. Then no matter how truly lovely it may be, it still should not be used as a container, for the attention of the beholder will hover between the vase and the flowers. The *objet d'art* should be set in its own suitable location where it can be freely admired for itself alone.

If you design a period arrangement and consequently must use a container expressive of an historic era, you may encounter some difficulty. Even when the period demands undisciplined contours or prodigal extravagance of ornamentation, you still must select a container that suggests the restraint of classic beauty; for intricacies of embellishment do not heighten the loveliness of freshly cut blossoms.

In working artistically with flowers, you have inevitably become highly color conscious. Most flowers, it is true, grow amidst green foliage; green is their natural environment. Yet you know well that green is not the only satisfying hue for a vase. You may choose at will from the entire spectrum, or from the neutral white, gray, or black.

You select the container for any given arrangement because you know that it is right for the floral picture you intend to create. You feel a comfortable harmony in the relationship of the flowers themselves, the design you will build of them, and the vase in which you will place them. If you wish to work in naturalistic style, your choice of container is limited. In material, color, and texture it must suggest the garden area from which the flowers came. Green leaf, brown branch, and gray bark—one of them will be right for the rough ceramic or the dried and weather-worn bit of wood you intend to use.

If you interpret the past, select an urn with rare sculptured qualities, perhaps, or a round or oval form on pedestaled base. You find intensity of color in pieces of Sèvres. Choose fine porcelain in white or ivory with delicate medallion imprints for daintiness, and alabaster with its wide color range—amber, brown, beige, powder pink, yellow, green, white, gray, and black—to express classic beauty.

Sometimes the size and texture of the flowers determine the container. Put large, bold blossoms in a vase of simple lines made from a material that suggests strength and stability.

All these examples illustrate what is meant by harmony of tone.

GLASS

The history of flower arrangement reveals a close connection between period trends in house design, together with furnishings and interior appointments, and styles of floral art. The most noticeable new development of contemporary architecture is the use of glass and plastic in actual construction and to make small articles for accessory decoration. Glass is by no means a modern novelty. It would be difficult to find objects more lovely than the Venetian and Bohemian glass of generations ago. But those intricately adorned pieces of art work stemmed from tastes different from ours. Our glass has been wrought into the same simplicity of form which distinguishes our other materials (Plate 119). The great sheets of glass walls are as unrelieved in their severity as the slabs of concrete or the bare surfaces of stucco that preceded them in architectural design. Though modern glass possesses the same strength to uphold great weight and the sturdiness to resist pressure of wind and storm which belong to the heavier materials of the past, it is yet as clear and as limpid as the goblets of the Venetians, and seemingly fluid in its rigidity. Glass containers of simple form display an extreme purity that often dismays the inexperienced arranger. At first you may encounter considerable difficulty in using glass containers because of that very transparency that gives them their singular beauty.

CONTAINERS

Glass containers range in price from the inexpensive to items manufactured solely for the luxury trade. The very costly pieces are too thick and heavy to be entirely satisfactory as containers. Glass can be so massive as to suggest a solidity of nature altogether at variance with your aim. You choose glass because of its sheerness, because you want a material so delicate as to be seemingly without substance. In selecting glass, then, do not be influenced unduly by name of maker. Select glass as you select ceramics or metal; that is, for basic forms of fine proportion with the degree of transparency necessary to heighten the loveliness of delicate blooms. Pieces of heavy glass whose beauty of workmanship makes them collector's items are, like ornate vases

PLATE 119

Coral-pink azaleas make up this arrangement for early summer. The container shares in the completeness of the arrangement. It is a beautiful piece of contemporary crystal, simple in line but very clear. To maintain the transparency of the receptacle with its water content the stems of the flowers are secured at the lip of the vase with a Y-shaped holder.

PLATE 120

*Epidendrum is a choice flower and Danish glass is equally
prized. The two specimens combine in a pattern whose aristocratic
tone is achieved by the simple placements of the orchid with uncluttered voids and the austere dignity of the container. The flowers are
vivid orange-red. The Y-shaped holder has been fitted at the water
line and is consequently concealed by the water itself.*

Precise placement has wrought spreading palm fans into a swinging curve with its implications of slender, sinuous beauty. This effect has been made possible in part by turning the fronds edgewise and in part by concealing a portion of the fans. Two strips of palm sheath form the tallest line. The foreground is filled with one gorgeous torch ginger, fully open, whose color extends to the top of the design in unopened buds.

of china or porcelain, so exquisite in themselves that they should be set apart and admired alone.

Plain and uncolored glass is the best choice for vertical containers. The water within the container will appear to increase the height of the glass and the length of the stems, thus magnifying the importance of the arrangement. The visible presence of the water is also desirable, since water is in itself attractive. When you admire flowers in an opaque container, you assume that water is present; but actually seeing it provides an additional, often unconscious satisfaction (Plate 120).

Glass containers other than vertical or pedestaled vases are acceptable, but they are not so flexible for general use. Bowls or deep plates are good for centerpiece arrangements or on low tables (Plate 121). The circle is always a unifying form for this type of placement; but novelty pieces, such as crescents, birds, shells, and the like, have limited use if made of plain glass. The same shape in other materials is more acceptable to the arranger's art. Simple forms in footed or raised glass are usually excellent. The stems and whatever else of plant material is below the water line are as much a part of the design as the material above the rim of the vase. That extension of design is one reason for the choice of glass as a container. The lower part of the composition is, then, more available to the observer if it is raised slightly above the table on a foot (Plate 122).

Beautiful as it is, glass is not adaptable to every setting. Glass containers should always be set where the light can shine through them. But if the light is not regulated, the surface of the container can look so shiny or glaring that the shape will become too obvious. Reflected light can be very unpleasant in a setting that is intended to be subdued and quiet. Remember, too, that functional glass suggests a contemporary setting. Glass of modern craftsmanship does not look too well in traditional rooms. It is the old principle of harmony—harmony of object and background. If you can have but few containers, you will find ceramics more useful than glass since they afford softer effects and unobtrusive textures to accord with any background.

FLOWER MECHANICS

In a transparent container where water is a part of the design, the water line must always be close enough to the top that the vase seems full (Plate 120). See that the water level does not change from day to day. If the container is not refilled, the ring left by the receding water is visible and untidy.

With transparent containers more than with opaque ones you must maintain a sparkling clearness of water content. Strip underwater stems of their foliage. Leave only the firm and tough stems for water immersion. Otherwise the rapid deterioration of leaves and other soft tissues produces an unpleasant discoloration. Plant tissues differ in their ability to withstand the disintegrating effects of water. Woody branched materials—such as flowering trees like plum, bushes like the rose, shrubs like the azalea—and the hardier, fibrous stems of flowers—such as the gladiolus and the peony—offer prolonged resistance to rot and its attendant water discoloration. Short-stemmed annuals disintegrate very rapidly.

Another enemy of water clearness is latex, a heavy fluid found in the cells of some plants. It is usually white and possesses more body than the watery juices of most flower stalks because of the numerous substances of which it is composed. It flows freely when the stem is cut and colors any water in which the stem is placed. Plants whose stems secrete this fluid should not be arranged in clear glass. But if one of the euphorbias must be used, allow the cut ends to bleed until the flow is exhausted. For this bleeding, place the cut ends in a water-filled receptacle other than the container to be used for the arrangement. This method is more successful, and certainly less troublesome, than siphoning off the discoloration and changing the water numerous times.

Probably the greatest challenge to the floral artist using glass is the concealment of objectionable stems. The presence of too many stems makes the base of the composition stuffy and reduces opportunity for reflections, prismatic interest, and sparkle which, after all, are the qualities for which the glass was chosen. One of the important principles of floral art is the elimination of crossing lines. The designer has learned long since to avoid such line placement above the rim of the container, but with an opaque vase he has never been aware of the nature of stem placement below water. Any attempt to cover up is likely to be disastrous. Do not use foliage, such as a large leaf, to conceal badly assembled stems. The only reason for introducing either

PLATE 121

Generously leaved sprays of variegated ivy mark the basic form of this design. In central position are full heads of pink dombeya blossoms whose delicacy is accentuated by the deep points of the encircling ivy. The container is a handsome piece of imported glass; the smoky black of the glass, together with its low, flat effect, gives a strong support to the spreading pattern.

213

PLATE 122

The vegetable garden can provide its share of refined beauty. This material is leaves of black chard trimmed in arrow-point lines at the tip. Enough of the blade has been left to show the startlingly brilliant red venation of stalk and leaf. The container of green glass has a molded recess in the center, like the cup of a candlestick, in which the leaves have been set. The contrast between the clearness of the vase and the boldness of texture and coloring in the plant material makes an arrangement of unusually dramatic strength.

leaf or flower within the container, and therefore under water, is that it may function as part of the design, as an arresting accent, perhaps, at the base of the composition. If the leaf is heavy textured, like the magnolia, or if the flower is unusually firm petaled and resistant to decay, very interesting etched effects are possible with an underwater detail of the pattern.

The holder may be as difficult to manage as the stems. It must not show conspicuously. The simple Y-shaped holder used for centuries by the Japanese is the best yet contrived for vertical effects when purity of line is desirable (Plate 123). Select a small crotch on the branch of a tree or shrub like a slingshot and fit the Y-shape in horizontal position to the top of the vase-opening. The size of the Y-opening is determined by the number of stems to be inserted. You can easily press the entire Y down into the mouth of the vase without any forcing. You will notice that the holder tends to slip down toward the bottom of the container instead of resting at the water line where it properly should sit. Knowledge of this fault is important for the beginner. If the holder is made too tight at first, after immersion it will swell and crack the vase. To prevent this breaking, place a bit of wadded cloth at the handle of the Y and compress it as the crotch is fitted and securely fixed. The cloth will not be visible but will serve as a shim to make the crotch firmly secure.

The stem ends of the flowers to be inserted in the Y are now cut on a slant so that they will rest securely wedged against the inner side wall of the vase. If they do not stay firmly upright, take a smaller flexible branch or stem and insert it outside and around the clustered stems so that it rests crosswise from vase edge, and north to south if the Y rests from east to west. This last limb placement is seldom needed since when the Y is firmly wedged with stalks, they bind and brace themselves to remain in place. In my *Flowers: East-West*, the technique of making and using this holder is pictorially illustrated.

If the plant material remains fresh, yet there is some water discoloration, just unclasp the entire unit of the Y holder, remove it from the vase, change the water, then reinsert the entire grouping. The lines of the arrangement will not be disturbed, since you have lifted the whole pattern.

Whenever it is desirable for stems to be viewed underwater, successful flower supports can be made of small twigs. Place several twigs wedged to form a lattice effect within the lip of the container at the water's edge (Plate 124).

Ingenious methods such as these will brace the stems or hold them parallel. Parallelism is highly desirable whenever the stems run the entire length of the vase and are exposed from the base of the container to its top where the floral cluster begins. Simple use of twig and branch is superior to the intricate contrivances of wire mesh concealed at the top of the container. When wire is secured firmly enough to hold flower stems precisely, it can scratch fine glass.

Plumber's lead is another aid. Make the arrangement. Then, holding it firmly in one hand, wire the stems together. Wrap the plumber's lead around this bundle of stems, leaving a short end that can be fastened to the edge of the vase at one side. This holder will not permit any of the stems to slip out of place, with a consequent alteration of the design.

For low containers or vases of varied shapes to which a lattice or a Y-shaped holder cannot be adjusted, the pin-type holder is recommended. Silver-painted holders instead of green ones are preferable, because they more nearly resemble the transparency and sparkling liveliness of water. If the pin-type holder is visible, it is so inconspicuous that it will not attract enough attention to itself to destroy the unity of the arrangement. The walled-type of pin holder should be used whenever the holder is to show, for the sides of the cup conceal the exposed needle points to the customary holder. Water is a magnifying agent that enlarges the undesirable as well as the beautiful. Visible needle points appear unduly large.

If you need a means other than these standardized holders, you must devise your own mechanics to fit your demands. As yet the market has failed to provide good usable holders for the numerous forms of transparent containers.

PRINCIPLES

Some glass containers are so beautiful that only floral treatment of striking simplicity or of great originality is suitable. Since the vase will be the basis of the design, the plant materials must not be permitted to detract from its distinction.

PLATE 123

*All the material in this design is elegant, and all of it is neces-
sary to produce the intended feeling. The table is Chinese of black
lacquer finish trimmed with a carved design inset with gold. The container is smoked glass, with the magnolia soulangeana held in place
by a Y-shaped holder.*

PLATE 124

This very simple design of roses placed in a clear, rectangular glass container shows how stems can be made an attractive part of the design. A lattice of twigs wedged at the top of the container holds the stems firmly parallel so that they become a necessary portion of the vertical placement.

In this circumstance employ a Y-shaped holder, for with this holder you can cut the stems so short that little of their length will show underwater. And you can easily conceal the shortened stalks by placing a leaf or a flower down over the container, or a cluster cascading in similar manner over the side. This floral detail not only conceals the mechanical support, but also produces transitional form between container and arrangement (Plate 119).

When an arrangement is made in heavier glass, where the receptacle is not the basis of the design but shares equally with the flowers in the finished portrayal, the stems should be visible. The stem structure, purposely silhouetted under water, serves to stabilize the design (Plate 122). Use a lattice holder when you wish to display the stems.

Since plain glass has no color, other than an occasional prismatic light effect, it does not affect the color pattern of the arrangement. When you select floral materials, ignore the vase in planning the color harmony unless the glass is colored. The hue of colored glass must be considered in the design.

The quality of the glass will help to determine the suitability of its floral content. A vase of extreme delicacy and grace, of thin glass and high polish, will be appropriate with such blossoms as valley lilies. For coarser leaves, flowers, or branches, use heavier, thicker glass forms.

Some flowers are set in plain glass because of their unusual sheen, their velvety texture, or their striking form. The native elegance of anthurium, ginger, magnolia, orchids, roses, tulips, and water lilies is heightened when they are combined with glass.

CERAMICS

Wherever there was clay, man made pottery for his containers. Where and when the first clay was burned, we do not know; it happened so long ago that it is lost in the abysses of time. The first and most primitive wares were unglazed. Most of the pottery we know is covered with a colored glaze, but this finish is also very old. Flinders Petrie, authority on the arts and crafts of ancient Egypt, has discovered that as early as 5500 B.C. the Egyptians used glazes, long before the Chinese, with whom the beginnings of the craft are frequently associated.

Ceramics will be your most useful containers—the easiest to obtain, they are also the most perplexing to select. The endless array of good and bad lines, the extremes of textures and glazes, the wide variety of colors; all this can easily bewilder you. You must remind yourself of the container's function and query its appropriateness to your setting.

CONTAINERS

Choose containers with the usual attention to thickness and weight. Thickness will range from the porcelain delicacy of fine vases to ponderous basins and urns. You need a variety. Delicate plants look their best in refined wares, in thin clay not so shiny as porcelain nor so dull as bisque. Clays of medium weight and thickness are safe for most plant materials, but very heavy bowls and odd pieces should be used only for cuttings with emphatic sculptural qualities (Plate 125).

Some ceramic pieces are unglazed; a few wear a partial glaze; most have a total glaze, though not always of high gloss. Vases of partial glaze are not always good for arrangement purposes because of their individuality. Like the unglazed pieces, they are likely to show too much of the natural clay color and its raw texture. You will prefer pieces of total glaze with their great range of hues. Since glazes are dull, highly brilliant, or finished with a blend of both effects, you can always find a receptacle to harmonize with the surface characteristics of your plants. The gloss of the anthurium matches the high brilliance of a bright glaze, and the dulled softness of a calla resembles the quiet mat glaze (Plate 48). A comparison of flower textures and vase finishes will help you to sense the satisfying harmony that can exist between flowers and a properly selected ceramic piece.

Avoid the extreme and the bizarre. Simple shapes are best. Do not become too enthusiastic over extreme sculptured ornamentation or other unusual textural effects. Appliquéd and over-decorative ornamentation of any kind is inappropriate.

FLOWER MECHANICS

Since ceramic ware is not transparent and very seldom fragile, you have little difficulty with the mechanics for floral support. A design of simple line set in a vertical vase can be held by the wooden Y-shaped holder. If the material is to be massed, use wire mesh. Vertical shapes with a mouth wider than the base, such as the urn, may be built up by layering cloth inside the container and then placing a pin-type holder on this padding several inches below the rim of the vase. This is an excellent method for employing the pin-type holder in any deep vase. When you set it near the top of the container, you can adjust flower stems horizontally—if you wish to make a triangular pattern in a classic urn. Although wire mesh is similarly adaptable, it is less clean and more difficult to manipulate than the raised pin-type holder. The pin-type holder is also good for low bowls. It should, however, be broad and heavy to support a large arrangement with many placements. If the holder is of proper size to hold all the stems, there is no reason to embed it in clay or melted paraffin.

Sometimes the bowl is so low that the holder shows. If you object to this detail, you can cover the holder. Work carefully, for the bowl must not look cluttered. Do not stuff fast-rotting material close to the surface of the water. Rocks, interesting tree formations, and other objects are much better for masking the holder than flower stems. It is far better to leave the holder exposed to view than to introduce a detail that calls attention to the attempt at concealment. The Japanese rarely conceal holders.

WOOD

Because of its texture, wood in the rough state makes extremely interesting containers for naturalistic arrangements. The Japanese always employ it for such purposes. They had noticed the textural surfaces of water-soaked boards and floating branches. Thus, they were inspired to devise containers formed from the wood of worm-eaten hulls of sunken ships and other underwater woods. The blanched and graying patterns of such cured wood make vases suited to the simple arrangements of the Japanese (Plate 126). Water-growing plants, such as reeds, lotus, and rushes are arranged in such containers. Sleek, finished bamboo also provides interesting color and texture. Portions of the stalk used upright or horizontally are easy to manipulate (Plate 127). Segments of bamboo are often used to cover an inner liner (Plate 128). Vases made of wood coated with lacquer are suited to the choicest flowers and foliage. The exquisite delicacy of the finish gives an elegant tone to lacquered containers.

METAL

The market offers a great variety of containers made of metal from the choice, but expensive containers of Japan to the familiar baking tins of our merchandise stores.

Silver is beautiful, yet it has many limitations. Constant effort is required to keep it clean and shining. The patina of age on copper and bronze is considered so desirable that the effect is often artificially induced—but not the blackened tarnish of silver. The greatest value of the silver container is for the centerpiece.

Silver, aluminum, pewter, lead, and tin are more suited for general color use than the warm metals of brass, copper, and gold. Although grayed metals are most adaptable to the cool hues of blue, blue-violet, violet, and red-violet, they may still be used successfully with the yellow to red-orange hues—for when interpreted as gray, they are neutrals that can go with any hue.

Textural compatibility between flowers and metals is even more important than color compatibility, for metallic surfaces are very conspicuous in an arrangement. Some silver has high sheen; other pieces are dull or powdered in effect. Tin has high brilliance, where pewter and lead are extremely subdued. Velvet-petaled blossoms belong in metal with a soft finish.

Brass, copper, and gold can be used only with flowers that have yellow in their hue: yellow-green, yellow, yellow-orange, and the like. Some cool colors may be used in the design, but only those that combine logically. In theory, brass is yellow; therefore violet, its complement, would be appropriate.

The more creative designers are using iron for containers or

PLATE 125

The blooms of the strelitzia nicolai are large and heavy with subdued tones of gray and black in the sheaths of the white blossoms. It is difficult to find a container of suitable weight and hue for such unusual flowers. This massive ceramic piece is correct in form and color. The simplicity of its lines properly subordinates its shape to the complex structure of the birds and therefore increases their importance. The color pattern is also improved by the container. The base and under side of the lip shade from gray to black, but are brightened by the glaze of the surface; the upper side of the lip shades from coral to gray. This coloring softens the sternness of the nicolai neutrals.

223

PLATE 126

Ranunculus blossoms are set in a container made from a small, hollowed tree stump. The informality of placement, much as if the flowers were still in the garden, is suited to the shape of the wood. The orange and yellow of the flowers is gay above the weathered gray of the wood.

PLATE 127

This design is as serene as an arrangement in the traditional Japanese style. Vivid red-orange clivia with its deep green foliage is the material. The most noticeable line is the long reversed curve made by the leaves of the two placements. Had one container been used, it would not have been possible to produce this sweep of leaves.

PLATE 128

Although this arrangement conforms to the principles of design, it has not followed set rules. The center of interest, the diagonal placement of birds of paradise, is high in the composition rather than low as is the custom. Vertical rods of equisetum and the small clump of iris leaves balance the vigor of the diagonal sufficiently to stabilize the design. Mats of baby-tears in the copper-lined bamboo container spill over the edge onto the table to increase the color interest and to heighten the illusion of birds in flight over a marsh.

226

as mobiles of free form with interesting textural finishes
(Plate 129). Some of these innovations are mere novelties. A
few are pure and beautiful, but many of them are inferior. It is
wise to move slowly among the unique shapes and those verg-
ing on abstraction.

BASKETS

Early civilizations did not use baskets as water containers.
They had baskets, woven of reed or grasses, used for storage
purposes. Baskets permitted easy handling of small articles. We
use them in this ancient manner, but we have also found a way
to hold water in them. If a water-holding liner is introduced,
or if they are sealed by a water-resistant varnish or plastic coat-
ing, they make charming flower containers.

Shapes are as varied as the materials to fashion them. From
the primitive workmanship of the peasant to the highest art of
the weaver—many kinds of baskets are available for container
usage (Plate 75). The refinement or the crudeness of the weave,
as well as of its material, will determine the plants to be set in
a basket. Weeds, grasses, and roadside flowers look well in woven
containers of simple form. The more refined and sophisticated
the basket, the more distinctive must be the plant material.
Since most baskets are in natural colors, they are suitable for
any color harmony.

PLATE 129

An arrangement planned specifically for placement in the modern home may use pieces of contemporary craftsmanship instead of the traditional figurine. Here a geometric form of polished brass occupies the central position in the design. Blades of New Zealand flax and fruits of the pomegranate are the two plant materials set in conventional pattern.

228

CHAPTER XII

Arrangements with Accent Objects

N̲O ONE KNOWS where or how the figurine first became associated with floral arrangement. It must have been a long time ago, long enough to provide grounds for conjecture. Painstaking investigation has given us a hint or two about figurines. In New York's Metropolitan Museum of Art there is a bronze flower bowl that was made probably a millennium and a half before Christ. It is a low, flat container with a shallow rim to hold water. In the bottom there is a device to hold flower stems in position, and mounted on top of this tricky holder is a small cow fashioned of metal. This basin with its tiny animal is valuable material for our speculations; for in Egyptian religion the cow was sacred to Hathor, the goddess of love, mirth, and social joy. She was often represented in Egyptian graphic art with a woman's body surmounted by a cow's head. The Hathor column used in Egyptian architecture has her face on the capital. The face is deeply sculptured and finished with a full, rolling hairdo that sweeps down below the cheeks to form the dentils of the capital. The face can be identified as that of Hathor by the ears, which unmistakably belong to a cow. So we find the symbol of a goddess in a flower container. After the floral material had been placed in the basin, the cow would look through the flowers or the foliage set around her. We use detached figures in exactly the same manner, for we often place them inside the bowl as well as standing beside it. It may have been the custom then to place floral or fruit offerings before the deity, coupled with a symbolic figure. This basin perhaps held offerings to Hathor.

The Greeks used wreaths and garlands to decorate the statues of their gods. This practice was continued in western European culture where, in the Middle Ages, elaborate and stately offerings in exquisite vases were set before statues and paintings of the Virgin. We have no record of medieval dining-tables that used floral decorations. Since medieval dining manners were of the robust and hearty type that required ample space for arm reach, it is extremely unlikely that there was either room or serenity for floral bouquets. In the warm summers, however, tables were often arranged outside. These seem to have been very elaborately decorated to suggest the landscape in which the fete was set. Not only were flowers used, but decorations were built with models of bowers or castles used in combination with flowers. French tapestries portray this custom.

The Renaissance custom of altar decoration has been carried down to our times. The statues of the Virgin and the saints that are the personalized symbols of faith are generally surrounded by flowers and foliage on feast days.

No wonder, then, that the floral arranger makes use of this custom. Flowers carried to place before the statue in a wayside or a garden shrine can have the same meaning if they are set before the image in a home, or on a table instead of in a niche. It is, of course, only a shifting of design to move the statue to a position in front of or beside the flowers. Worship might not dictate the second placement; but it is not an irreverent position, and if the statue is St. Francis, it is an exceedingly logical location for the saint who held out his hands to welcome all tender, lowly creatures.

With the development of interest in flower arrangement these statues have multiplied. Their subject matter has been extended beyond church drama and liturgy to include the entire world of lay interest. This wide field of selection has led to a certain amount of confusion that calls for clarification on the proper use of such forms.

The greatest offense has been the employment of figures in a manner unrelated to the plant material, to the composition, and to the setting. You should, above all, appraise the form you intend to use and be sure that you understand its meaning. If it is a Madonna, the flowers must be suitable to interpret purity. From the beginning the lily has been the Virgin's flower. An arrangement of lilies, then, is the true expression of spiritual tradition (Plate 94).

If the figure is St. Francis, tradition again suggests the proper association. When we think of the Saint of Assisi we remember his meditations and his sympathy with birds. A composition may employ branch or foliage rather than flower forms, for he is represented as walking under the trees when he came upon the birds (Plate 130).

Since these two figures are almost always vertical forms, they dominate the setting. Any plant material will be subordinate to the symbolism of the statues. Plant material may surround them or be clustered very simply in the foreground.

An angel will be given altogether different positioning. Angels are subordinate figures in religious paintings. In the "Annunciation" of Martini the angel is as large as the Virgin and as near the center of the picture, but the positions and the facial expressions of the two figures clearly indicate the subordination of the angel. In most such paintings the Madonna is given the central position, and the angels are unmistakably to one side or vaguely above in the air. Angels are not individualized personalities; they are symbolic adornment. Therefore in a flower arrangement the angel will share importance with the flowers or even be of secondary interest in design. Angels require a setting of delicacy; the floral material should be frail and tenuous to suggest their ethereal nature. Their body forms of soft, curved lines, their flowing draperies, and the feathery lappings of their wings establish the lines of the floral arrangement (Plate 95).

Other than religious subjects, any figure—real or imaginary—that completes your floral idea is suitable. You should give the same expert appraisal to human, bird, animal, fish, or insect forms that you give to the religious figurines.

A dominant vertical form placed in the arrangement is actually a substitute for a piece of floral material. Use it in the same manner (Plates 94, 131). You may also set a vertical form parallel to a line established by some other feature of the design to emphasize through repetition (Plates 3, 4).

You will discover that a vertical figure may be used properly when it is an integral part of the design, when it continues a line, or when it is a substitute for a line. In any of these ways it helps to formulate the pattern for the design.

Whenever the figurine displays softened contours and circular motion, plan a design to effect rhythmic repetition of its lines.

Textural delicacy of a lacelike figurine, such as the Dresden piece, immediately suggests textural forms in dainty floral material (Plate 97).

A seated or crouched figure shares in, or is subordinate to, the design. Structurally, it lacks any dominance of line unless it is of massive proportions, such as a seated Buddha. A Buddha could dominate by its personality, regardless of position. It would somewhat approximate the significance of the more usual religious figurines. The seated figure will contribute additional interest to the composition when you use it to continue a line or where you need a mass to fill a large or uninteresting space (Plate 132).

The texture of the accessory determines the plant material. Delicate floral material is not texturally suited to a ribbed statue with heavily folded draperies. Use strongly veined foliage to accent some small detail in the design that would otherwise go unnoticed. In Plate 132 the venation repeats the folds in the garments of the figurine.

Arched shapes in the accessory are highly desirable. They combine the strength of a vertical with the added grace and smoothness of the circle. Because the lines are primarily vertical, they can serve all the purposes of a pure vertical, even to replacing plant material in the design.

In Plate 133 the desirability of the arching vertical is evident in the Venetian artist's conception of the massive fish. Your trained eye will see a vertical line from the tip of the tail to the heavy base on the table. Therefore the arranger could have made the fish dominant in the design by eliminating some of the heavy plant material. You can use an accessory with as much distinctive quality as this fish in various ways. You can set it upright and silhouette it with foliage; you can place heavy-petaled flowers low at the base. In this pattern the extreme heaviness of the glass has a remarkable textural sympathy with the fibrous but sleek surface of the agave.

Horizontal forms are also effective for compositional purposes

PLATE 130

Leaves of the jacaranda tree surround the figure of St. Francis. The fernlike quality of this foliage makes it highly suitable to suggest a garden or a forest setting for the contemplation of the monk. The material, set in a pin-type cup flower holder, is so manipulated that it conceals the manner in which it is secured.

PLATE 131

In this arrangement two figurines are featured. Since they substitute for a vertical floral line, the composition would have been a
rather uninteresting diagonal with no particular vigor of motion without them. Now it is stabilized as a triangle. The figurines are set at
unequal heights just as floral lines differ in length. The colors are
dramatic: the figurines with their yellow kimonos; the yellow Peruvian
lilies with their brown fleckings; and the gorgeous tiger lilies.

PLATE 132

A seated Oriental figure in robes of green and brown, holding in his hands a vivid orange persimmon, sits beside an earthenware jar. The container holds three large strap leaves of crinum, set with their backs to the observer to show their heavy venation, which is similar to the textural pattern in the folds of the garments of the seated figure. Brilliant tiger lilies supply the color needed to brighten the pronounced browns of this study.

PLATE 133

    The accessory in this design is as interesting as the plant material. The glass fish is dramatic because of its shape and the semblance of muscular tension. Its color of blue-green banded with silver bears a remarkable resemblance to the grayed blue-green of the agave leaves; and the edge structure of the agave leaves has an equally unusual likeness to the finned silhouette of the fish. This is a very lively design.

236

because, like the vertical figures, they too can establish lines for the pattern or become a part of the design. Use a crouched lion or a pheasant to establish the horizontal line. Then set a vertical placement of plant material to make the composition a triangle.

In other words, use the vertical and the horizontal figures in exactly the same manner as plant growth. Whenever figurines appear, they must become a part of the design. They should not be stuck into or beside an arrangement that is satisfyingly complete without them.

The color of the accessory is important. It must combine with the hues of the plant materials to build an acceptable color pattern.

If you see in your accessories the same qualities that you discern in your plants, you can weave them into delightful patterns.

CHAPTER XIII

Dried Plant Material
and other
Lifeless Forms

IF YOUR MAIN INTEREST in plant design lies in composing patterns of floral color, the barrenness of your garden in winter need not dismay you. You can keep your home gay with flowers if you know the methods of preserving plant material. You must, first of all, understand which varieties are best suited for preservation; and then learn the processes of drying.

Flowers called "everlasting" are old-time favorites in home gardens. Straw flowers, globe amaranth, yarrow, statice, and others last almost indefinitely when made into bouquets. In addition to these, nearly all garden-grown varieties can be dried to retain their hue. The color is sometimes as vivid as when the plant was growing. All colors can be secured, even brown, which is rare in natural flowers.

Dried materials are valuable because they are durable and economical; but, like most expedients, they have limitations. They do afford decorative pattern, which is the principal reason for their use, but they cannot replace the beauty of cut plant material. One evergreen branch effectively arranged means far more than meticulously set spikes of dried larkspur. One medium reveals the vigor and the beauty of living things; the other exhibits only a decorative appeal to delight the eye by form, line, texture, and color—or as a conversation piece. Both media are suited to the floral artist, but in different ways. When you resort to preserved materials, you should regard them as a reserve force to provide a decorative note during the barren portion of the year. But even then you should use them sparingly.

Some dried materials are suitable at all seasons of the year. Arrangements of dried reeds, leaves, branches, grasses, seed pods, and berries are good at any time because we do not have the same kind of emotional reaction toward these parts of plant growth which we experience with flowers. We admire them as we admire stumps, driftwood, rocks, and other objects that are always present in the landscape. Therefore when used for arrangements they imply naturalness. Even snow-covered fields in winter hold small patches of dried growth. But to employ dried pink peonies with dried orchid hydrangea blooms at this time of year is a different matter. These are summer blossoms. They do not belong with winter chill. Because of the warping of seasonal habits this sort of design becomes merely an accessory to other objects permanently and naturally a part of interior decoration (Plate 134).

The perfect dried floral material to combine with winter reeds and grasses is the last blossoms of autumn: celosia, calendula, dahlia, Chinese lantern, marigold, statice, yarrow, zinnia, and chrysanthemum. Gracefully and quite logically they extend the beauty of autumn through the chill months preceding spring (Plate 135).

Leafy branches and cut, large-bladed leaves are your best source for dried material. They have longer lasting-quality than other floral materials. They are easy to manipulate and do not resent the roughness of ordinary handling. When the drying process has been completed, they more honestly approach natural beauty than fragile blossoms do. The process itself can be managed without any equipment. When the stem ends are placed in water, they eventually will absorb the entire water content of the receptacle. If no additional water is provided, the leaf blade will gradually dry to the same color that it would have reached if allowed to die naturally in the garden. The garden specimen drying on its stalk is more fragile than its artificially dried counterpart because it suffers from the wind. Since each leaf or branch retains its individual shape, this latter drying method can be applied to leaf material in an arrangement. Think, then, of the possibilities in an all-green arrangement of aspidistra leaves. In a low container holding water they will be fresh and attractive for months. Then they will dry a natural brown; and, with some shrinkage in size, they will retain their form and the positions in which they were set in the original arrangement (Plate 136).

Sometimes you prefer a result that the drying method cannot give. You may, for example, want a different tone value: perhaps an intensity of brown which you cannot obtain by the above-mentioned method; or a natural green; or red. You may even want a quality other than color, such as a greater pliancy with little shrinkage. In any of these events, use the glycerin method.

GLYCERIN TREATMENT

Glycerin treatment is recommended for the foliage of trees that retain their leaves for a prolonged period—the magnolia, for example. Preserve only the leaves of deciduous trees, not the leafy branches.

The formula for the mixture is one third glycerin to two thirds water. Mix the solution well and place in a jar. All plant material to be treated must be free of dust, blemished leaves, and infected leaf areas. Cut the stem end vertically several times; or, if it is very tough, pound it with a hammer until the inner stem cells or fiber are exposed. Place the plant cutting in the solution, with at least a five-inch immersion of the stem.

A period of two to five weeks is required to accomplish much change, the length of time determined by the variety of plant growth. When the solution has been fully absorbed, the leaves will have changed their color. The color change is gradual, and you can determine the progress by checking the tip end and the leaf edges. If they are not sufficiently colored, encourage a freer flow of the fluid by recutting the stem ends and allowing them more time to absorb the liquid. Different tonal effects can be secured, depending upon the time the material has been immersed. Mottlings which often appear midway in the process can be very attractive. You can secure all-over hues of green or

PLATE 134

This design of dried floral materials is primarily a harmonious color study. Several methods of drying were used. The spikes of purple larkspur were scattered on newspaper and allowed to dry in a shady location. The two peony blossoms and the hydrangea heads were hung upside down for the drying process. The very realistic pansies were treated with borax. The colors make an analogous harmony ranging from blue to red-violet.

241

PLATE 135

An interesting tree form offers protection through its distortion to the last remaining seed pods and flowers of autumn. The form of the tree determined the placements of the wild dock and the barley stalks in a slight curve to repeat the heavy arc of the tree. The disk forms of the strawflowers echo the circular pattern of the design.

242

PLATE 136

This is an all-green foliage arrangement that was placed in water where it remained fresh and attractive for several weeks. As the water was absorbed and decreased, the plant material gradually dried out. It retained its original shape even when lifeless, but its color changed to soft tones of brown. This one composition, then, afforded two altogether different concepts. The green aspidistra, the magnolia, and the rubber leaves offered refreshing beauty. Now lifeless, its beauty comes from its form. Dogwood blossoms treated with borax have been added to embellish the design.

red or yellow—and tints or shades of yellow or red are possible—
if you remove the leaf at the right time.

You must modify the process for some few materials because
of their growing habits. Earth-clinging plants, for example, absorb moisture through the under pores of flower or leaf. When
you condition the flowers of such low-growers as violets and
pansies, you must immerse them completely before you attempt
an arrangement. In like manner, any earth-clinging foliage
plants such as ivy, galax, and ferns react more favorably to
glycerin treatment when given total immersion in the solution.

Use the glycerin method under all conditions and at all seasons of the year. To freshen glycerin-treated materials, wipe
with a warm, moist cloth. Or, if too delicately foliated for wiping, the leaf material can be placed in kitchen or bathroom and
steamed by running the hot-water taps.

Foliage Treated in Glycerin

ASPIDISTRA	LAUREL
AUCUBA	LEUCOTHOE
BARBERRY	LOQUAT
BEECH	MAGNOLIA
BIRCH	OLEANDER
CRAB APPLE	ORCHID TREE
DRACAENA	OREGON GRAPE
ELAEAGNUS	PHOTINIA
EUCALYPTUS	PITTOSPORUM
FORSYTHIA	PRIVET
GALAX	RHODODENDRON
HUCKLEBERRY	SAXIFRAGE
IRIS	SEA GRAPE
IVY	VIBURNUM
JUNIPER	YUCCA

BORAX TREATMENT

The borax method is suggested for the preservation of some
blossoms with fragile texture. It requires less time than other
drying methods, but demands close observation of the materials being treated. They will disintegrate if allowed to remain
in the borax too long.

The usual procedure is to line a box with paper and add powdered borax to a depth of three or four inches. Next, defoliate the blossoms and see that they are completely dry before placement in the borax. Spiked flower forms are laid parallel and not touching; disk forms are set upside down with the flower head supported on the borax. Sprinkle and work the borax gently around the petals until the entire blossom is covered. Fragile flowers require about twenty-four hours for preservation. Some heavy blossoms take much longer. Any flower difficult to preserve because of its delicacy may react favorably to this method.

Flowers Treated in Borax

ASTER	GLADIOLUS
BALLOON FLOWER	GLOXINIA
BALSAM	IMMORTELLE
BLEEDING HEART	KNIPHOFIA
BUDDLEIA	LILAC
CANDYTUFT	LUPINE
CANTERBURY BELLS	MARGUERITE
CARNATION	NARCISSUS
CHRYSANTHEMUM	PANSY
CLEMATIS	QUEEN ANNE'S LACE
COLEUS FOLIAGE	ROSE
CONEFLOWER	SPIREA
CORAL BELLS	STAR-OF-BETHLEHEM
CORNFLOWER	STOCK
COSMOS	SUNFLOWER
DAFFODIL	TULIP
DAHLIA	VERONICA
DAY LILY	VIOLA
DEUTZIA	VIOLET
DOGWOOD	WATER LILY
FOX GLOVE	ZINNIA

SAND TREATMENT

Some authorities prefer sand to borax. The method of operation is the same with both media and the results are similar.

Other experienced workers dislike sand because of its weight on frail bloom.

NATURAL DRYING METHOD

Commercial flower growers who supply dried flowers to the retail trade use a very simple method. They treat only materials in prime condition. The flowers are defoliated and dried of all moisture. Then they are suspended, floral head down, from a wire line. Some varieties are bunched. Peonies and hydrangeas must be hung separately instead of being bunched. Hardy varieties commonly treated for the commercial trade are statice, straw flowers, celosia, yarrow, and others. Since the recent introduction of the bells of Ireland (Plate 137), this flower also has been treated. The florist has not extended his selections to more delicate species because of the shattering of petals in the handling necessary in the merchandising process.

Some workers use a less-formal method of natural drying which has been very successful. They scatter the flowers loosely on spread newspapers, then leave them outdoors in the shade. The flowers suffer less shrinkage and less shattering than when suspended; they finish the process with purer colors. Naturally, both of these results add to the beauty of the material. Larkspur, watsonia, marigolds, and a large number of other garden flowers react favorably to this casual method.

If you demand a nicety of detail in color and texture, use the natural drying method, for you can depend upon it for securing uniform results.

Naturally Dried Flowers, Foliage, and Plants

ACACIA	BIRD OF PARADISE
AGERATUM	BITTERSWEET
ANTHURIUM	BOUGAINVILLEA
ARTICHOKE	CALENDULA
BABY'S-BREATH	CASTOR-BEAN PODS
BANANA LEAVES	CATTAIL
BARLEY	CECROPIA
BAYBERRY	CELOSIA

CEYLON MORNING-GLORY PODS

CHINESE LANTERN

CLOVER

CORN

CUPID'S-DART

DELPHINIUM

DESERT HOLLY

DOCK

DUSTY MILLER

EUCALYPTUS PODS

EVERLASTING

FALSE DRAGONHEAD

FALSE INDIGO

GAILLARDIA

GENISTA

GERANIUM

GINGER PODS

GLOBE AMARANTH

GOLDEN ROD

HEATHER

HELICONIA

HOLLY

HYDRANGEA

JACARANDA PODS

LARKSPUR

LAVENDER

LEMON LEAF

LIATRIS

MAGNOLIA PODS AND BUDS

MARIGOLD

MILKWEED

MONTBRETIA

MORNING-GLORY PODS

MULLEIN

NANDINA BERRIES AND BLOSSOMS

NEW ZEALAND FLAX

OATS

ONION

PALM LEAVES, CALYX, SHEATH

PALMETTO

PAMPAS GRASS

PANDANUS

PEONY

PEPPER-FRUIT PODS

PLANTAIN

POMEGRANATE

POPPY PODS

PUSSY WILLOW

RHODODENDRON PODS

RUBBER PLANT

SAGE

SCOTCH BROOM

SMOKE TREE

SNOW-IN-SUMMER

STATICE

SUMAC

SWEET SULTAN

TEASEL

VERBENA

WATSONIA

WHEAT

WILD-CUCUMBER PODS

YUCCA PODS

YARROW

Always select floral materials just after it has opened sufficiently that the petals are dilated. Be sure that spiked forms are not shattering when picked. Completely defoliate the stem, then cut and place in water for reviving. When the bloom is crisp and fresh, remove it from the water and wipe it thoroughly. Although any water absorbed through the stems in the freshening state is helpful, moisture on the petals is damaging to the drying process.

Select branches from shrub or tree for interesting line. When nature does not provide interesting variations from the normal line of growth, artificially shape the material prior to drying by bending, tying, or wiring the branches into such forms as you need for purposes of design. Pussy willow, aspidistra, genista, and Scotch broom can be easily curved preliminary to drying (Plate 138).

Expect a certain amount of shrinkage to occur in the drying process. This is especially noticeable in flowers. Therefore, when composing designs, use three or more dried flowers where you would use one in fresh condition. Also, set them closely, leaving fewer voids within the frame of the design. The main placements of the pattern must establish firm contours of clear-cut form (Plate 139). Otherwise the arrangement may appear cluttered. This sharpening of line is also necessary to clarify the color pattern, since the muted color values predominating in foliage and branch lessen the contrast of hues always apparent in fresh material (Plate 140). A composition consisting primarily of dried flower forms attracts the eye because of its color. Be careful with color arrangements. Preserved flowers lose their hue very rapidly if exposed to direct sunlight or if set in brightly lighted rooms.

Select containers to suit the delicacy or the heaviness of the dried material. Fragile and lacy forms belong in fine porcelain or delicate glass; solid forms with firm contours, in pottery, wood, or metal.

SKELETONIZING

Sometimes you want an arrangement so lacelike that no foliage is sufficiently delicate to suit your purpose. Then you use skeletonized leaves that look like framed shapes of patterned air. The fleshy part of the leaf has been removed, leaving only the complex network of veins.

Sturdy leaves of hard texture are suited to this treatment. Avocado and magnolia leaves are favorites. Besides their firm texture, they have handsome shape bounded by crisp contour lines, and they are easily obtained. Select perfect specimens.

PLATE 137

 *This design affords an excellent example of the combining of
materials for their form and texture. Tall stalks of acanthus and bells
of Ireland, both treated by the hanging-upside-down method of drying,
enclose one dried frond of the embryo palm. A chain woven from disks
made of reeds is caught onto the acanthus and hangs down to enclose
the rosette forms of the bells of Ireland. In this monochromatic design
the plant materials are pale beige.*

PLATE 138

Four willow twigs have been manipulated into soft curving lines while still green. Although originally arranged in water, they were removed prior to the swelling of the catkins and allowed to dry out completely. The tip end of the magnolia branch was treated with glycerin to give it resilience and a varied brown tone. Although these leaves will dry naturally, they are more brittle and much more likely to tear than when treated with solution. The daffodils and their buds were treated with borax.

PLATE 139

Two leaves of dried aspidistra dominate in this design of dried materials. Palm spathes of similar shape are used for container and basal emphasis. Four umbeled stalks of agapanthus, two spikes of torch ginger dried in its natural color of coral-pink, and the rounded forms of wood rose establish rhythm through disk forms. One dried and furled leaf blade of pandanus connects the tall vertical and the long horizontal lines.

PLATE 140

Three dried leaves of the bird of paradise are impaled on a pin-type holder so that their attached stems contribute to the design. The brown pottery container through its crescent shape suggests the repetition in the leaf and the stem placements. Two dried blooms of the bird of paradise are featured for silhouette. Rounded forms of the leaf of the sea grape which have been treated with glycerin unify the pattern and conceal the holder. This composition has none of the cluttered effect often seen when dried materials are used without concern for their silhouette or the individual form of each unit of the material.

252

Blemishes will be even more noticeable after this treatment than when the leaves are dried; spots on the skeleton will destroy the illusion for which the phantom forms were made.

Wearing gloves, since the solution is caustic, combine one pint water, four teaspoonfuls lye, and one half pint Clorox. Bring to a boil. Add the leaves. Boil until they are limp but not soft. Run cold water into the container to reduce the temperature. Remove the leaves, scrape gently with a toothbrush, then rinse under tap water. If any flesh remains, scrape again. Press between paper towels to dry. Though the leaves will look as frail as gossamer, they are remarkably strong and will stand a good deal of use. You can keep them with the white effect of the bleaching or dye them to gentle pastels.

In addition to plant materials that can be processed to serve beyond their normal life span, nature offers an abundance of objects that can be worked into beautiful arrangement patterns. Rocks, driftwood, bark, tree stumps, roots, coal, shells, and the like are good as accessories or even as the basis of the design.

ROCKS

Rocks are always interesting because of their rich venation or mottling, their color, and their shape. For generations the Oriental has set them apart in his garden, enjoying them as much for sheer aesthetic delight as for the part they play in his religious beliefs. We employ them in our landscapes for their native beauty: we set them in artificial pools and on embankments; we even create rock gardens. The flower arranger can use them in designs to suggest, at least in part, the beauty of the natural scene.

Rocks whose shape resembles any basic geometric form present an interesting point of departure for floral design. Stand a tall, vertical stone in a low bowl, with violets or valley lilies grouped as in true growth at its base. Use rounded rocks with echeveria or any disk flower to create a spectacular abstract design. A triangular grouping of plant material with a triangular rock at the base makes a strong composition (Plate 43).

Small pebbles and stones are excellent accessories. If they are placed for repetition or emphasis and follow an established line of the pattern, or if they supply a line, taking the place of plant material, they are an integral part of the composition (Plate 141). Small stones of similar color and shape may be scattered under water in a broad, low bowl or placed like stepping-stones to break the water level. They may also be used for the entirely practical reason of giving mechanical support to plant material or of concealing the holder.

Color range in rock and mineral forms is as wide as the differences in weight and texture, from the dark gloss of coal to the delicate tints of quartz; from the deep brown of rock to the colors of patterned marble or the striated gray of granite. The arranger has unlimited opportunities for the inclusion of stones (Plate 142).

DRIFTWOOD, BARK, STUMPS, BRANCHES, ROOTS

The silver sheen of sun-bleached wood very easily becomes the basis for beautiful composition (Plate 4). You can find pieces of driftwood sculptured by nature into fantastic shapes that will build dramatic patterns; or aged wood whose deep serrations add quiet and stability to a design.

The burnished glow of a polished burl or the sleek lines of a peeled branch add smart touches to conventional arrangements. Furled strips of bark serve many purposes. Properly placed they can make rhythmic transitions; as vertical placements they are splendid supporting-lines. Set in horizontal position they function as container (Plate 74). Even a tree stump has its use (Plate 126).

If branches or bark are covered with lichen, so much the better. They are all the more expressive for realistic designs, especially if the wood is combined with plant material. The Japanese make fine use of lichens and wood in their naturalistic scenes.

Combinations of weathered tree stumps or roots with rocks are exceedingly useful in creating patterns intended to simulate an intense emotional reaction, particularly the ideas of loneliness or desolation.

PLATE 141

The extreme simplicity of this arrangement of iris leaves and wild grasses is intended to express the peace of nature. The wisps of plant material, the glass disks, and the rhythmic pattern of the pebbles all contribute to the grace of the composition.

PLATE 142

A *study notable for the distinction of its materials uses yellow callas and glass. The blossoms are strikingly tinged with green on their outer surface. Were the flowering stalks eliminated, the foliage would be excellent material for leaf arrangement through the beauty of its white mottlings against the vivid green. The piece of glass slag is luminous and vividly yellow, exquisite when used alone for specimen material or when used, as it is here, for color unity.*

If you have no driftwood, you can achieve the driftwood finish artificially by bleaching a piece of wood in water to which salt has been added, or by applying gray, flat-finish paint and wiping it into the crevices.

CORAL AND SHELLS

Materials from the sea have many decorative possibilities in their form, texture, and color. They can function as the basis for design, as background, or as container. They can establish a marine theme in which they either are featured or appear as accessories in the design. All too frequently the designer uses such objects indiscriminately, without proper attention to similarity of association through shape, line, or environment.

When you employ them to establish the mood of a marine scene, the only suitable pieces are those that belong to such an environment. Grasses and rushes, driftwood, seaweed, or any shoreline growth are logical combining-material. If you wish to combine coral and shells with a few blossoms, you should remember that the form of a flower is far more important than its color. Use a rounded shape for such a design, because you add the blossoms for accent, setting them low in the container as if you had employed the sea anemone, which you are trying to suggest (Plate 143). Blossoms from the cactus family or the water lily with delicate waxen petals and long stamens seem to be floral counterpart of those delicate sea creatures with their incredibly exquisite flower form. Many shells are so beautiful in shape or texture or color that they provide decorative treatment in themselves (Plate 144). To feature the specimens, select plant material of equal distinction (Plate 145).

Unpolished shells are porous; therefore, it is possible to intensify or alter their color. Any liquid dye wiped on will color shells, but coral must be immersed in the dye solution.

All of these lifeless forms are interesting because they are novel. They can be worked into attractive designs, and they are always evidence of the skill required to produce them. But they never can replace the beauty of one living piece of plant material.

PLATE 143

    Two shells are placed side by side, with one large spray of fan coral extending on the left to suggest a radiating form of composition. One aloe plant is centered at the base, selected for its shape and its spiny fringed leaf blades that suggest the starfish. Because of this detail it seems at home in its undersea setting.

258

PLATE 144

In this fantasy of the sea the rippled edges of four wands of shimmering golden plastic suggest the motion of waves. Maidenhair fern, bleached, colored ivory, and dried, resembles underwater plant material. Glass balls encased in wire mesh sparkle like bubbles ready at any moment to rise to the surface of the water. The shells are from the Philippine Islands.

PLATE 145

Two golden shells have been so highly polished that they are almost luminous. Three blue-violet water lilies show a center of vivid yellow beneath the delicate maze of their stamens. They look like fragile creatures of the sea, like the flower forms of the sea anemone. This is, then, a true harmony of shell and flower.

260

CHAPTER XIV

Japanese Miniature
Plant Art Forms

BONSAI

ONE OF THE features of Japanese garden art which attracted the attention of Western garden-lovers is the dwarf or stunted tree. Purely Oriental in its inception and development, it aroused not merely curiosity, but profound wonder. That a fully developed tree one hundred or more years old can exhibit every characteristic of ripe maturity, yet be only inches tall, seemed at first too unreasonable for belief.

Such a tree today is known as a *Bonsai,* a word that means roughly "planted in a shallow pot." It is not an ordinary potted plant; it is a tree that, if left to itself in its natural environment, would have grown to normal proportions, but it has been artificially dwarfed through a very long and careful cultivation. Unremitting daily attention for endless years has been necessary for the production of these refined works of art.

The first Bonsai seem to have been cultivated in Buddhist monasteries. The oldest recorded pictures of such potted trees are contained in the thirteenth-century scrolls that describe leading events in the life of Honen Shonin, one of the founders of Buddhism, who lived probably in the twelfth century. Later, in the seventeenth century, the serious cultivation of miniature trees began. For a time the chief purpose was to produce something misshapen, so extreme and fantastic as to be, at times, even grotesque. But fortunately the Japanese love of exquisitely fine proportion put aside these crippled specimens. Since that time the effort has been to create a beautiful work of artistic realism. As in all features of Japanese gardens, the Bonsai suggest far more than they visibly express. The observer who studies these Bonsai is expected to picture to himself an entire landscape.

Bonsai have different shapes in accordance with different characteristics of the trees. Four main classifications indicate the shape of the tree trunk:

(1) *Chokkan* is the upright trunk of a tall tree that stands in a level field probably surrounded by shrubs or trees of lesser growth. The foliage of this specimen will be approximately symmetrical (Plate 146).

(2) *Shakan* is the slanting trunk of a tree that grows on a sloping hillside. The foliage here will be heavier on one side than on the other because of the differing exposure to light and air (Plate 147).

(3) *Hankan* is the gnarled trunk of a tree that has grown for years on a cliff. Twisted and gaunt, it has braved the buffeting of the winds, but its warped body testifies to the bitterness of the effort.

(4) *Kengai* is the drooping trunk of the tree that overhangs a cliff. It is rooted, perhaps, in a crevice, or clings precariously in unstable footage; yet its whole downswept length exhibits a marvelous vigor and the will to live (Plate 148).

The basis of this classification is a natural one, for the trunk is the most important feature of the tree. Many fine specimens have more than one trunk growing from the base. There may be two, three, five, or more than six trunks; but never four. Some pots contain a small group of trees of one or several varieties (Plate 149). This grove effect is also produced by causing several trunks to rise from one long horizontal root.

The trunk must exhibit an unmistakable truth to nature. Inevitably it will be short, since full-grown trees are usually under three feet; but it must not look chopped. It must not seem to have been topped to shorten it; the trunk must taper gradually, with branches of appropriate length and thickness.

The size of the leaves and the fruit cannot be materially reduced. For this reason the small-leaved trees are better subjects for Bonsai treatment than broad-leaved trees. This principle is very apparent when the tree has reached advanced maturity.

PLATE 146

The ginkgo is an easy subject for the beginner in Bonsai. That
it can maintain its growth under adverse conditions is probably the
reason for its survival from the remote past. The maidenhair tree, as
it is popularly called, is one of the most ancient plant forms extant.
Along with the ferns, which also grew in a dim geologic age, it links
us with an epoch so removed that trees, as we know them, were only
in their infancy. A true denizen of the Orient, it grows happily as a
Bonsai specimen. This pattern exemplifies the two-trunk tree type.

PLATE 147

    This seventy-three-year-old pine tree, only eighteen inches tall, displays every evidence of age. Because it has been unable to grow upright, the slanting trunk is so heavily branched on one side that the dense twig system with its thick mat of needles almost obscures the cones. The visibility of the roots offers further proof of advanced maturity. Rocks have been added to increase the realism. Had more emphatic shaping been given to the root stock to develop a decided twist in the main trunk, then it would have exemplified the Hankan type of tree.

PLATE 148

*This juniper could have been a shapely tree had not circum-
stances forced it completely out of symmetry. The two branches on
the right side of the trunk show its effort to assume a normally upright
position. The Bonsai-maker has shaped it in the Kengai fashion, where
the trunk droops almost to the ground. Were this tree completely to
taper over the container, the tray would be placed on a tall pedestal,
truly expressing the fourth type of distortion—as if drooping over a cliff.*

265

PLATE 149

   The yeddo spruce is a favorite subject with Japanese Bonsai artists. Three tiny trees have been allowed to grow in the Chokkan pattern. Careful manipulation has induced gentle curves in the several trunks so that, though they grow upright, they do not in any way duplicate tree design. Since each tree has its own graceful pattern, there is no monotony. The shrines of Japan are planted with the yeddo tree. Thus it is a reverential subject to the Japanese.

266

Because any aged tree has an extensive twig system, the branches of the Bonsai display an intricate network of twigs at their ends.

Next in importance to the well-branched trunk is the visible root system of the tree. Roots that emerge from the ground, at least in part, give a semblance of solid support. Because roots are flexible, they can be manipulated to differing positions and directions of growth. They can be trained to extend almost to the limits of the container before growing down. The Japanese often introduce a stone at the base of the tree, close to the trunk, and shape the roots to grow over the sides of the stone, as if clasping it, before they enter the ground. These high, bare roots clinging to the stone increase the illusion of insecure footing on a mountain slope. Any basal network of roots produces an effect that in natural growth could result only from age-old living. The tree in Plate 147 is seventy-three years old.

The Japanese find some of the subjects for Bonsai treatment growing in the mountains where the plants have been so handicapped by their surroundings that they have not been able to grow normally (Plate 148). Perhaps they have been caught in rocks or are so crowded and cramped that they have been stunted from birth. If these trees can be removed without too much injury, they make splendid Bonsai material. But more often the root system is too badly damaged for successful transplanting. The usual methods of starting Bonsai are to use cuttings, to graft, to layer, or to plant seedlings. If the Bonsai is to represent a majestic tree, a cutting one inch in diameter with proper care will root. Grafting is less often used because the grafted joint is too likely to be visible. Layering is often employed if one is in a hurry to get the tree started. Growing from seed, though probably the slowest method, is often the most satisfactory because the tree can be shaped from the start.

The choice of container in which the Bonsai is to grow is an important matter. It must be chosen not for its beauty but for its suitability for the particular tree that lives in it. It may fit no other Bonsai, but if it is harmonious with the form, the size, and the shape of its occupant and heightens the beauty of the tiny tree, it is the right choice. Because the Bonsai is intended to create the feeling of landscape, the container should be in earth tones rather than brilliant colors. As the tree ages, it must be moved to a container that is an antique or that has been treated to suggest the mellowness and the ripeness of old age.

The container is prepared with a slight amount of soil, the least possible to maintain healthy living-conditions. It must be a soil that will admit air freely and hold moisture. The Japanese use a hard-clay soil that can be worked to a fine powder, then add a bit of loam, some sand, and leaf mold or peat moss. Even so, the Bonsai must be watered regularly whenever the soil becomes dry, perhaps twice a day in warm weather, perhaps as many as five times. In cooler seasons, particularly in the spring when plants normally put out a vigorous growth, the Bonsai should not be heavily watered, for profuse watering will stimulate a too vigorous growth and excessive foliation.

Even with the best of care the tree outgrows its container. The food supply of such a small amount of soil as that provided for the Bonsai is soon exhausted. Inevitably the tree becomes root-bound. Transplantings, then, are necessary. When the tree is lifted, the mass of roots is gently broken apart so that part of the old soil may be removed. Then the roots are pruned, freely if the tree is young, very slightly if the tree is aged. For continued growth the plant must have healthy roots; therefore root-pruning carefully done is one of the important features in assuring steady development. During this process the plant must be protected from exposure to extreme light. Unusual air conditions, either of sun or wind, can easily be disastrous to the delicate root hairs unaccustomed to harsh atmosphere. Transplanting usually is done in the spring. Conifers are transplanted every four or five years, but fruit trees more frequently. Some growers recommend annual transplantings for flowering-and-fruiting Bonsai.

Twig-pruning is essential for Bonsai to stimulate branching and to retain the form that the grower desires. The young shoots of coniferous trees are pinched back, leaving only a little bit, perhaps a quarter of an inch, at the base from which the needles grow. The shoots of deciduous trees are pinched to leave two buds at the base. Flower buds are retained, but leaf buds are nipped off, keeping only enough to give the tree the form that the designer is cultivating.

The natural pruning given these trees is much like the pruning done in any garden or orchard, except that it is more severe. This pruning, however, is not the kind that gives the Bonsai its individualized form. The culture of a good Bonsai requires trimming or dwarfing of a particular sort that demands great skill. In Japan professionals can be hired to trim Bonsai much as Westerners employ landscape architects. Their work is so expertly done that few, if any, traces are left when the trunk has been topped or branches have been removed or shortened. These artists take pride in the realism of the effects that they create. Even when they bend stems or branches, they are producing one of the natural tree forms. The bending is done by wrapping insulating wire around the branch to be shaped, then gently forcing it into the desired form. Months later—usually six months to a year—the wire can be removed, but the branch will retain the form indefinitely. The direction of the bending is customarily down, then outward, for this is the position of the branches in many naturally aged trees.

Bonsai require fertilization because of the austerity of their soil. A manure of slow effect is preferred to a chemical fertilizer because the tiny trees will grow so vigorously as to lose their character as Bonsai if overfed.

Many Western trees are suitable for Bonsai specimens. The Monterey cypress greatly resembles the Ming tree that was an Oriental favorite from the fourteenth to the seventeenth century. Most conifers, such as pine, juniper, spruce, fir, cedar, cypress, and yew, are easy to manipulate. Among the broad-leaved trees Bonsai are made from bamboo, ginkgo, elm, beech, maple, and willow. Bamboo is the plant for the beginner. The root system is exceedingly hardy, and the tree is exceptionally vigorous in its will to live. Even if dried out, it will persist (Plate 150). The ginkgo (Plate 146) is also easy to do. Fruit trees—lemon, orange, cherry, persimmon, crab apple, apricot, peach, plum, pear, and quince—make likely subjects. Flowering trees and plants—azalea, hawthorne, dogwood, camellia, honeysuckle, magnolia, rhododendron, and wistaria—can be wrought into charming effects.

Bonsai trees are now so generally admired that they are found in botanical gardens in Western countries. As yet, few persons cultivate them at home because the development and care of a good Bonsai require more time than the average family wishes, or can afford, to give. Unless they are given daily attention of a very particular sort for years, they will either wilt or grow out of bounds. But the few people who choose to work with this Oriental art create specimens of unique beauty.

BONKEI

Another miniature form in which the Japanese delight is the tray landscape, or *Bonkei*. Like the Bonsai, this tray form is apparently of religious origin. In the early stages the sacred earth forms associated with Taoism or Buddhism were reproduced on trays. The picture scrolls of the thirteenth and fourteenth centuries which record events in the lives of Buddhist saints show neatly planted shallow boxes near the shrines, with tiny trees and mounds that suggest hills and mountains.

The end of the nineteenth century marks the beginning of the modern tray landscape, which is an art form with none of the early religious significance. Today the middle classes of Japan delight in this form of nature representation. Several schools of Bonkei, each with its own principles and techniques, conduct classes for those who wish to practice Bonkei-making as a hobby.

The Bonkei-maker creates an interpretation of nature which is not only attractive but also revealing of the close association between man and nature. The subject matter is much the same as that found in Oriental paintings: mountain ranges; paths leading into mountainous country; water falls and mountain streams; cultivated fields, perhaps with suggestions of agricultural activity; beaches with fishing villages, or seascapes with typical tides and surf; historical scenes. Sometimes a foreign scene of great international interest is worked out, such as Niagara Falls or the Sahara; but the typical Bonkei deals with landscape as the Japanese know and love it (Plate 151).

The building of a tray landscape is not difficult. The tray itself is usually rectangular or oval, one to three inches deep. Large trays measure one by three feet; small ones, six by eighteen inches. All sorts of material are used—concrete, metal, wood, pottery, porcelain. Each of these has its particular advantage. The cement basins are very durable; furthermore, they can be colored to fit the design. Wooden trays have a natural harmony

PLATE 150

Bamboo is dear to the Oriental heart. Consequently it is a splendid subject for Oriental treatment. This specimen, though twenty-one inches tall, is actually only five years old. Because of its hardy root system, careful manipulation is required to retain it in a bowl of any kind. This bowl, deeper than the containers used for most Bonsai, is intended to keep down the necessity for too frequent root-pruning.

PLATE 151

This Bonkei shows beautifully the three-dimensional feature that makes the tray landscape a highly successful interpretation of nature. In the background a waterfall from a high mountainous crag forms a tiny stream that empties into the river flowing past the peasant home. A laborer approaching the bridge gives a very realistic human touch to a scene that is picturesque with its rocks, some moss-covered, its cryptomeria, and the accent of gay color in its flowering trees.

272

with the subject of landscape. Metal trays, usually brass or bronze, are great favorites. They are used in instruction work because they are inexpensive and light to handle. There is a great variety of pottery and porcelain trays, many of them very expensive.

The artist uses peat or newspaper pulp for the landscape. The best peat contains a large amount of silicate. Because these deposits are limited, extensive experiments have been made with other materials, the most successful being with rough paper. Newspapers are cheap and easily obtained in large quantities. The sheets are crumpled, then placed in a container. Boiling water poured over them reduces them to a sticky ball that, when cool, is kneaded into a solid mass to be manipulated much like modeling clay. It is next wrapped in absorbent cloth and squeezed. After all excess water has been removed, the pulp is mixed with powdered acid-clay to give it sufficient body to retain its shape. If the artist uses peat instead of paper, this same clay is mixed into the peat and kneaded smooth.

After the material has been prepared and is still moist, the landscape is shaped on the tray according to a previously sketched design. The shaping is done with strokes of a spatula, not in too great detail since the mountains are supposedly viewed from a distance. Natural color effects are obtained with powdered pigments applied with a brush; the colors used are principally light brown, red, and green. Touches of blue and violet indicate distances between mountains.

Water is represented by colored sand sifted thickly on bare spaces in the tray. Enough water is poured over the sand to cover it, and the surface is smoothed with a paintbrush. After the surface has been leveled, any water remaining is removed with a syringe. Waves or ripples are made by thin lines of white powdered marble. Waterfalls are usually painted.

Tiny grasses, bits of evergreen material, patches of moss represent natural growth. The plant material may be real or artificial. The market is rich in supplies of miniature objects made with Oriental precision of detail. Tiny plants and trees, scaled to fit the proportions of the trays, help to create the illusion of great distance in these three-dimensional pictures. Easily obtainable also are tiny buildings typical of Japan—shrines and temples, castles and homes of peasants, all of baked clay—ships, rafts loaded with merchandise, fishing boats complete even to the fisherman with his net; then people and animals. The objects are beautifully wrought by competent artists who specialize in these creations.

When the tray is completed, it must be kept moist to retain its color and form. Then it is set in position to be admired, usually as an ornament for the alcove.

CHAPTER XV

Trends in Flower Arrangement

RENDS IN floral composition follow trends in other art forms. Any attempt to discuss what is happening in the field of flower arrangement must first take into account what has happened to the setting in which the floral design appears. For any floral arrangement in a house is a decorative detail. The room is functionally complete without it. If the architecture is modern, the house is probably low and well spread-out. Though it may not be large, it will seem large. Flat boundary walls without too much interior partitioning create the semblance of spaciousness. Great picture windows and sliding walls of glass extend the room to the terrace beyond. Mirror walls multiply the actual space and add a pretentiousness perhaps unwarranted by the actual dimensions.

The furnishings establish the tone. Rooms identical in construction to the last modern detail can be made altogether different in spirit by their furnishings. However unlike the furnishings may seem, they will be akin in their simplicity, their functionalism, and their air of uncluttered space.

One room may have furniture of metal and glass: glass-topped tables supported by standards of steel and iron; chairs with metal frames; lamps on metal pedestals. Such a room is coolly sophisticated.

Then substitute wood furniture. It can be quite as contemporary in design as the metal and the glass; it will be blond or bleached. Yet the difference in tone is immediately perceptible. Countless generations of mankind have furnished their houses in wood. The very idea of wood inevitably suggests the associations traditional with home. This room is as smart as the first one and as competently modern, but its refinement is not brittle. The change in atmosphere has been effected almost entirely by a change in texture.

For a third approach, suppose the designer goes further and introduces figured ornamentation: he covers one side with figured wallpaper, hangs a tapestried panel or a large landscape mural; supplies figured window drapes or chair covers. Even a very small amount of such decoration will temper the extreme modernity of the architectural design. Accessories and flower arrangements that truly belong in room one or room three might be used in room two, but would seem out of place if interchanged.

Modern living accents speed and efficiency, both of which create strain. We overemphasize the dynamic and the mobile. As we meet the stresses that impinge upon us from all sides, our life becomes a drama of escape. This feeling of drama is being expressed in plant arrangement. Simplicity, functionalism, drama: these are the keys to modern floral arrangements.

Not all homes are of the so-called modern architectural pattern. Beautiful new homes exemplify the best in the past, and are furnished in keeping with their period. But they are not homes of bygone eras transported from ages ago. These homes are as comfortable, as convenient, and as lovely as their contemporary neighbors, and wonderfully interesting; for they make us feel the traditions of the past while maintaining the excitement of the present. And they, too, display much of the simplicity of the modern pattern. They require fewer and less-colorful arrangements than were made in the period itself. The classical urn lavish with flowers was a favorite, perhaps, in the traditional home (Plate 11). The modified period home prefers the grouping of a few tulips in a luminous container (Plate 47).

DESIGN FOR THE CONTEMPORARY HOME

The structural design of the contemporary home has completely shifted the emphasis of plant interpretation. Flower arrangements are seldom used unless the blossoms are distinguished by unusual color or form (Plate 50). Shapes found in highly individual flower heads are right; the geometric pattern of the globe artichoke or its cousin, the wild thistle; the seed-forming disk of the domestic sunflower; or the exquisitely pendent billbergia—all serve admirably in contemporary design (Plate 152).

Contemporary architecture deals with flat, unrelieved planes. It presents great inset expanses of stones; it uses solid timbers, grained or deeply serrate. These attributes of strength encourage the use of conspicuous compositions: floral patterns employing large-headed blossoms or designs composed entirely of foliage or branches. The new houses use foliage in large planters. Or they employ foliage unrealistically for dramatic pattern effects much as the arranger has always used cut blossoms (Plates 153, 154).

Perhaps these unusual foliage designs will displace blossoms for interior decoration. It is possible that flowers arranged alone may be used only for accent effects and for special occasions. This trend will not in any way interfere with their acceptance in the traditional way when a floral pattern is desired; nor will it indicate their disappearance from homes of traditional design.

You have a ready substitute in your garden and the knowledge wherewith to use it. For your plant education is not limited to flower forms only. Before you studied flower arrangement, you had gained horticultural information through experiences in your garden which made you familiar with foliage and branch. Not until you had learned all three—branch, leaf, and flower—did you feel equipped to study modern floral design. Consequently you are aware of developing structural forms in your garden and alert to their possibilities as decorative material. You have seen the vividness and the subtlety of color in leaf and stem; you have pruned and shaped the fine edges and planes of contour in twig and branch; and you have fingered their texture. Complete in this understanding you realize the value of foliage plants in building compositions of permanent decorative value.

CONTAINERS

In this new trend the plant material and the container share equal interest. This principle is contradictory to the older approach where the container was usually subsidiary. These containers are selected because they seem to be a part of the house rather than vases to hold plant material (Plate 155). Accessories are highly original, often hand-wrought. The decorative value of the pieces are sufficient without added floral interest; they can function with or without flowers or other plant material (Plate 156). When the pieces are used with floral design they are still important, and the arrangement merely shares in the sculptor's artistic expression (Plates 157, 158).

Arrangements of today are far more original than those of the past. If you have a facile imagination, you can make astonishingly novel designs (Plates 159, 160). Consider a few examples of current change. For your contemporary home you can make a foliage design in raised and patterned relief (Plate 153). The simplicity of overlapping lines and bladed form is strongly effective against the modern wall. Use direct application of foliage or tree branches in pattern, or unusual driftwood forms in silhouette (Plate 153). If you do not care for direct application, try a design of cut foliage, rhythmically composed of overlapping segments (Plate 154). It is stylishly beautiful in its simplicity.

THE FUTURE

For your contemporary home you may want to experiment with a kind of design that seems entirely new. You can build patterns that at first glance appear to belong more to a scientific than an art world because of their novel materials and extremely free use of space. Both Japanese and Occidental designers are working with these new concepts. Criticism of Japanese floral art has been directed chiefly at its inelasticity, because it has been purely symbolic and limited to a design invariably triangular in pattern (Plate 27). The leaders of the new movement in Japan are the former teachers and associates

PLATE 152

Billbergia is startling in form, in texture, and in color—excellent plant material to express the unusual. Billbergias belong to the pineapple family; and the common variety, of which this one is a specimen, grows in the garden in many areas in the United States. Related species are collector's items in hothouse settings. The long pink stems grow tall; the buds slowly open to suspend tasseled clusters in yellow-green and cobalt blue. The fantastic color combination and the unusual spiked form lend distinction to anything with which it is associated. Two giraffes abstractly carved from burnt wood repeat the color of the charcoal pottery container.

PLATE 153

This is an example of plant material appliquéd on a plain surface when undecorated wall spaces may be embellished by a simulated
bas-relief. For durability glycerin-treated magnolia leaves have been
fashioned into the shape of one large leaf by the successive overlapping
of leaf on leaf. This shingling conceals the thumbtacks used to fasten
the leaves. Stalks of banana sheaths make stems to unify the three
placements as one group.

PLATE 154

Segments of sheaths of the trunk of the banana tree have been
peeled one from the other and arranged with simplicity and precision.
An arrangement of this type gives excellent patterned relief to a wall
space where a painting or similar ornamentation would not be desirable. A single leaf of the cut-leaf philodendron conceals the holder and
repeats the fluted columns.

PLATE 155

For the contemporary home where accessories of simple, classic beauty are desirable, an Oriental container is appropriate. It offers the same spareness of detail as the architecture and is made of fine, strong material. A bronze usubata holds delicate sprays of equisetum, arranged for the etched effect of their lines. The bronze crayfish repeats the same qualities of beauty by the fineness of its bodily form.

282

PLATE 156

Two ceramic dancing figures have been given sufficient contemporary treatment through angular expression of body contour and arms to accord with other highly modern furnishings. These large figures should be used with plant material in suitable proportion. Young shoots of the large bamboo are placed erect in the manner of true growth. The discarded covering-sheaths from the same plant are overlapped to form a triangle that unifies the composition as well as giving it an almost theatrical effect.

PLATE 157

The great advantage of foliage is its availability throughout
the year. Not only is it desirable in winter when the barren season is
at hand; but equally so—yet frequently overlooked—during the hot
months when the gardens of the great Middle West are depleted. In a
pin-type cup holder concealed by a Japanese tree slab, two branches
of a miniature variety of juniper are placed naturalistically. A tiny
Japanese fan has been set as if artlessly tossed down to complete the
mood of the composition.

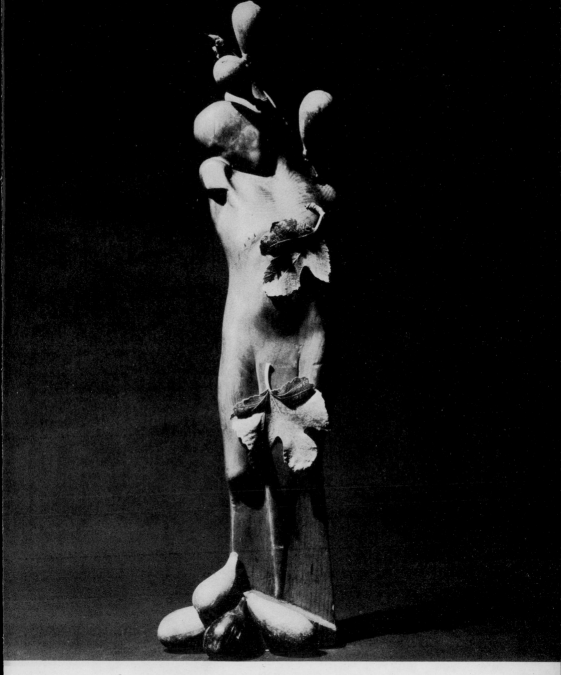

PLATE 158

    *This plate shows a modern design created to feature the statue
alone. The vertical figure is complemented by placements of plant
material repeating curves within the form of the sculptured piece. Fig
leaves and fruit illustrate the flexibility of contemporary trends.*

285

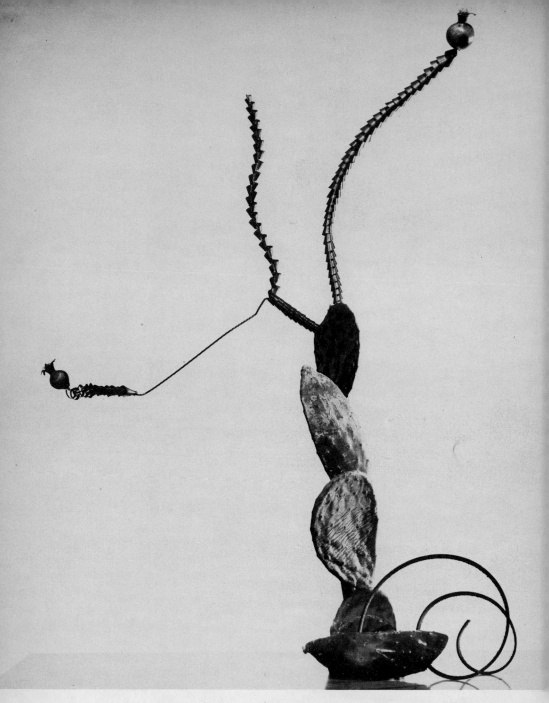

PLATE 159

Metal lathe-turnings and cactus are the materials of this design.
It complies with the present trend for furnishings and accessories of
metal to use in the modern home. Two small fruits of the pomegranate
are impaled on the tips of the extending arms. Whenever plant material is used with this type of abstraction, it is selected not only for form,
texture, and color, but also for durability, because the pattern seldom
offers a possibility of placing the plants in water.

PLATE 160

Mobiles make impressive decoration for plain surfaces or wall areas or empty space. Whenever modified to permit the addition of plant material, this trend has its particular importance for the floral artist. Bark-strippings from the eucalyptus tree are highly adaptable for purposes of spare design. One miniature sedum rosette rests on the crossbar. Other sedums are located at the axis of the pattern.

287

of the traditional schools. They are working now with patterns that completely disregard any symbolic factors and that indicate their interest in contemporary scientific and industrial progress (Plate 161).

American designers have made more progress than the Japanese toward the free use of space. The work of Alexander Calder shows what can be done with spatial conceptions of abstract design. His training as an engineer led him to work with metal. From thin strips and plates of metal bent into free forms, from pendent wires and lacings, he has created mobiles of delicate adjustment which are set into motion by air currents. As they move, they carve rhythmic and involved patterns of space which become a fluid part of his design. In combination with these fine bits of metal he uses solid objects for accent—croquet balls, pieces of glass, and driftwood.

The artist working with plant material always makes use of any new trend in contemporary art. This abstract manipulation of wood and metal, this prodigal employment of space has established a point of departure for original designs in plant arrangement (Plates 159, 160, 161, 162). You can take the simplest geometrical forms and the most severe plant material. Without any attempt at ornamentation you can set these materials in position like blocks hewn from space. The resulting composition is as new as contemporary abstract sculpture, and it is very interesting (Plate 163). It is the kind of composition, perhaps, toward which the Japanese have been working, but which they have not clearly realized.

For while the United States has been developing these new and sensitive designs of pure form and line, the Japanese movement has sheered away toward the grotesque. The unpleasantness of Japanese representation shows most clearly in their containers and accessoriés. Japanese containers have been notable for their exceptional beauty. Now the traditional containers with their beautiful contours and lovely proportions are no longer employed. Nor is any attempt being made to modify modern floral composition to permit their use. Contemporary containers have assumed amazing proportions and abrupt form. Those constructed of pottery are extremely crude, too heavy. They lack the harmonious relationship of shape and weight which we have always associated with Japanese ceramics.

Some arrangers employ containers suggestive of human forms.

A container sculptured in crude clay will suggest the hips and the legs, exaggerated in grotesque fashion, with plant material held in the top of the form and arranged in a mound. Another container is vaguely reminiscent of a human body, with armlike appendages but no head. A few blossoms are used for the face so that the whole implies form completion.

All these are quite dreadful. In contrast to the development of these bizarre containers is one fine aspect of the Japanese movement. The Japanese designer is experimenting with abstract composition, using such materials as iron rods and coiled wires. His patterns exemplify to a remarkable degree the good third-dimensional form for which the Japanese have always been noted, and some of his achievements are mobile effects much like those of American artists.

Wood is also used, not necessarily as a container, but as the basis of a design or as an accessory. Lifeless tree trunks, branches, and piled-up twigs are preferred to living tree growth. Plant materials new to the Oriental and now employed are sea kelp, aerial mosses, cactus, and succulents.

No floral designs of great beauty have as yet been observed in the compositions of the advanced movement in Japan. It is unlikely that there ever will be anything that we can consider particularly desirable, since the Japanese arranger is completely untrained in Occidental interpretations of art. Our principles of design are so different from Oriental concepts that a comparison cannot be made.

The Oriental does know line and form and at times expresses them more adroitly than we do. But in his new interpretive approach he has completely lost his feeling for floral color, proportion, scale, rhythm, and texture. He combines the heavy, unwieldy form of the globe artichoke with the delicacy of baby's breath. He assembles these unrelated plant materials in placements almost defiantly antagonistic to any compositional plan; then he sets the grouping in a heavy vertical container.

His feeling for interesting texture and form in wood is a basic heritage that the Japanese will never lose. By his free use of this material he is making an excellent contribution of great universal appeal (Plate 164). His other interpretations may at times be interesting; but his accessories frequently overpower floral design.

This movement as yet has not matured. Given time for improvement, it can be the means toward a refreshing new form of floral approach. Both the East and the West are breaking away from imposed restrictions. Americans, particularly, are creating with fluid unrestraint. The artists of plant design have all the other arts to help them. They can make use of every modern concept of form and space composition. They can find beauty in every natural fragment and fashion it into realistic or abstract design (Plate 165).

PLATE 161

This geometrical design replaces a painting of humanistic representation when the decoration of a room is cold and severely modern. Plaster-of-Paris forms and one dried umbel of roadside grass are the mediums used.

PLATE 162

The mature floral artist can shape his plant materials into symbolic design. The tall form represents humanity; the smaller form, continuity and reproduction. Spanish moss entwines man and forever chains him to his world. The eye means man's forethought and vision.

292

PLATE 163

Geometrical forms can contribute just as importantly to exciting and dramatic pattern as do lifelike reproductions. Simple blocks are the basis of this design that is meant to encourage the floral artist to develop a facile manipulation of material.

PLATE 164

This reproduction of a modern Oriental design is an excellent example of the newer trend. The Orientals are using woods of distinctive shape and texture for composition embodying geometric form. The spiraled iron depicting the motion of the sea is boldly three-dimensional. The contemporary home in America can make use of similar patterns as relief from the older driftwood hangings.

294

PLATE 165

An unusual branch of wood, weathered and bleached, has been sandblasted smooth by the winds of New Mexico. Even a sluggish imagination can see a pitiful figure wretchedly trudging across the desert wastes. Spanish moss tops the head and makes a threadbare drapery for the body. White pebbles and white sand at the base suggest the original environment.

INDEX

i

A NOTE ON THE AUTHOR

J. GREGORY CONWAY *was born in Billings, Montana, in 1909 and is a graduate of the University of Osaka in Japan. Now widely recognized as America's outstanding floral designer, he is equally expert in the classic modes of the Orient, in the freer style of the West, and in his own adaptation of the Eastern technique of flower handling to our native flowers and to the vast array of containers of modern design. He was the first Occidental to hold a diploma from Japan's famous Ohara School for the Moribana and Nagiere styles in flower arrangement.*

After his return from Japan, Mr. Conway was chosen by the University of Southern California to give accredited art courses in flower arrangement. He also acts as floral consultant in a private capacity, and is widely known throughout North America and Europe as a lecturer and demonstrator. Mr. Conway is the author of CONWAY'S TREASURY OF FLOWER ARRANGEMENTS, FLOWERS: EAST-WEST, *and* FLOWERS: THEIR ARRANGEMENT.

A NOTE ON THE TYPE. *This book is set in* ELECTRA, *a Linotype face designed by* W. A. DWIGGINS (1880–1956), *who was responsible for so much that is good in contemporary book design. Although much of his early work was in advertising and he was the author of the standard volume* LAYOUT IN ADVERTISING, *Mr. Dwiggins later devoted his prolific talents to book typography and type design, and worked with great distinction in both fields. In addition to his designs for Electra, he created the Metro, Caledonia, and Eldorado series of type faces, as well as a number of experimental cuttings that have never been issued commercially.*

Electra cannot be classified as either modern or oldstyle. It is not based on any historical model, nor does it echo a particular period or style. It avoids the extreme contrast between thick and thin elements which marks most modern faces, and attempts to give a feeling of fluidity, power, and speed.

The book was composed by WESTCOTT & THOMSON, INC., *Philadelphia; the text and black and white illustrations were printed by* AFFILIATED LITHOGRAPHERS, *New York; color plates printed by* KINGSPORT PRESS, INC., *Kingsport, Tennessee; binding by* H. WOLFF, *New York.*